pisces
prediction
Astrology
Aquarius

planetary ascendants
solstice
Mercury

Christine Grenard

CASSELL&CO

Mayan cosmology is based on three calendars designed to harmonise actual time, the solar year and the movements of the heavenly bodies.

 27

47%

of middle and senior executives believe in astrology, compared with 36% of the population as a whole.

 41

63%

of people believe that personality can be explained by star signs.

 41

The traditional *Yi Jing* draw

performed with fifty *achillea millefolium* sticks, which are separated and sorted several times.

 97

The four perinatal matrices

By linking the four birth phases with the four planets – Neptune, Saturn, Pluto and Uranus – a person's dominant characteristics and qualities are revealed and placed in context with the great myths and the phases of human development.

 98

111 theses

relating directly or indirectly to astrology were published in various universities throughout the world between 1905 and 1998. 38

Mars in Capricorn

achieves goals with perseverance and control.

 107

Dragon

fiery, strong and independent – a winner.

The doctor, **alchemist**, astrologer and seer, **Nostradamus** used **astrology** to devise his prescriptions; he foresaw meteorology, developed **remedies** from plants and wrote his famous **prophetic quatrains** (*Astrological Centuries*, 1555). Many of his **predictions** came true, both during his lifetime and after his death. ▶ 30

In the 1930s, Dane Rudhyar, an American composer and astrologer, studied the notion of temporal cycles and identified the influence of the Moon and its phases on human actions.

 32

Pluto travels around the zodiac in 248 years, Uranus in 84 years and Saturn in 29 years. In the birth chart, the movements of the planets have a triggering effect and the major events in a person's life generally accompany them.

78

The Moon, the Earth's satellite, sets the rhythm of our days and nights and plays an important role in the birth chart of an individual, as it does in nature in general. With its short cycle, the Moon's influence is associated with mood changes and daily preoccupations, explaining the origin of terms such as 'lunatic'.

 72

Yi Jing
The Book of Mutations or Transformations

The *Yi Jing* is used by the Chinese for divination and is based on the interplay of yin and yang, which, in combination, are at the root of the existence of all beings.

97

Simplified draw

Throw the coins six times: the number of heads and tails obtained each time corresponds to a yin or a yang trait.

97

NYD
Temperance

WYNN
Joy

GAR
Harvest

**an introduction to
Nordic runes** 82

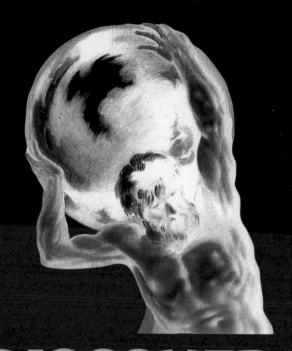

DISCOVER

THE FIRST ASTROLOGERS AND THEIR METHODS OF PREDICTION.
THE LINKS BETWEEN ASTROLOGY AND ASTRONOMY.
SUPERSTITION AND HERESY IN THE MIDDLE AGES.
ASTROLOGY IN THE AGE OF AQUARIUS AND THE NEW MILLENNIUM.

Since Mesopotamian times, mankind has looked for connections between celestial phenomena and human events on earth. Astrology, the practice of interpreting the influence of the heavenly bodies on mankind, was originally linked to astronomy, the study of the constitution and movements of the heavenly bodies. However, from the 17th and throughout the 18th century, when science and logic came to the fore, the two fields of study were separated, with astrology increasingly regarded by many as mere superstition unsubstantiated by factual evidence. But at the end of the 19th century, the influence of astrology began to reassert itself. The work of astrologers Alan Leo (1860–1917) and Sepharial (1864–1929), founding fathers of the Astrological Lodge of Great Britain, greatly contributed to this. The 20th century saw its popularity increase. In the USA, Paul Clancy embarked upon a mission to popularise astrology in the 1930s, and Dane Rudhyar created the daily horoscope. In addition to this, the influential Swiss psycholanalyst, Carl Gustave Jung, used astrology in his studies and wrote extensively on the subject. At the beginning of the 21st century, a growing awareness of the potential for environmental disaster along with rapid technological development means that science alone no longer seems to provide all the answers, and interest in astrology continues to grow.

THE POLITICAL INFLUENCE OF THE EARLY ASTROLOGERS

The Sumerians, ancient inhabitants of Lower Mesopotamia and inventors of cuneiform writing in around 4000 BC, engraved clay tablets with symbols representing the positions of the Moon. Traces of these, dating from the seventh century BC, and of translations of even more ancient tablets, have been found in the library of Assurbanipal in the ancient city of Nineveh in present-day Iraq.

MELSHIPAK II

From its earliest origins in Mesopotamia, astrology influenced the power of sovereigns, as demonstrated by this 'kuduru', which was found in the tomb of King Melshipak II (c. 1100 BC).

The Mesopotamians believed that the Earth and the sky were created from the body of the goddess Tiamat (the sea), which in turn had been divided in two by Mardouk, one of the first great Mesopotamian gods. According to their beliefs, earthly events mirrored what was happening in the heavens.

The planets were considered to be incarnations of the gods. The most important, Sîn (the Moon), a male god, had three children, two of whom were Shamash (the Sun) and Ishtar (known to the Romans as Venus), also called the 'Queen of the Heavens'. Mardouk (Jupiter), who distributed tasks to the other gods, and also played an important role.

The gods were revered in daily life and were the focus of public worship. It was believed that they sent messages to Earth in the form of celestial phenomena, such as comets, the phases of the Moon, eclipses, and planetary conjunctions, which the astrologer/priests (known as *baru*)

ATLAS

Mythology, geometry and astrology: a major trio of Antiquity symbolised here by the giant, Atlas, condemned to carry the heavens on his shoulders.

were called on to interpret. Their forecasts were very much concerned with the big picture – the future of their kings, the people and even the land itself. They referred also to the constellations, which were used to provide a scale of reference for accurate measurement of the Moon's position. The astrologer/priests throughout the country kept note of anything out of the ordinary (on earth as well as in the skies), believing that, should any strange phenomena reappear, the events accompanying them would also recur. They recorded their observations on tablets. The ones relating to celestial occurrences constitute the *Enuma Anu Enlil* collection, which contains numerous detailed predictions, such as: 'If there is an eclipse on the night before the month of Aiar, the King will die and the King's sons will accede to their father's throne'. If bad predictions were made, the people prayed to the gods in the hope of mitigating the impending disaster. Since eclipses were generally considered to be unlucky, the King was often replaced by a substitute until the danger had passed. The unfortunate substitute monarch was then executed. According to the records, it seems that this occurred quite frequently.

The priests, who were also the King's advisers, had a direct influence on the country's politics. During the first millennium BC, they no longer limited themselves to observing and interpreting the heavens, but took advantage of the development of mathematics and the measurement of time to calculate in advance the positions of the planets and stars at any given time. They plotted these positions precisely on a band of eighteen constellations – the precursor of the twelve signs of the zodiac, which was developed in around 400 or 500 BC. This marked the birth of what we now call astrology, along with its predictive methods. The first known individual horoscope dates from 410 BC. From this point onwards, astrology was no longer limited to kings and queens, anyone could make use of it.

The borders between ancient kingdoms were in a constant state of flux, and when Alexander the Great made territorial gains in the middle of the fourth century BC, creating numerous colonies throughout the Near East, the local cultures fell under Greek influence.

ASTRONOMY, ASTROLOGY AND GREEK MYTHOLOGY

Astrology flourished in Greece and was closely linked to religion and science, as demonstrated in Plato's *Timaeus*. This book describes the creation of the universe in the form of a sphere by the Demiurge (the specific Platonic term for 'creator of the world'). He positioned the planet gods, who reigned over the animals of the zodiac, along the ecliptic (the Sun's path and the line along which eclipses could occur). These planet gods, or rulers of the zodiac, were thought of as spiritual powers, and each individual 'soul' could choose which of the twelve gods to follow, their degree of divinity being dependent on their position. The basis of modern science dates from this period. The work of Pythagoras was very influential, as was that of Aristotle (who defined the four elements: fire, air, water and earth; and the qualities: hot, cold, dry and wet, that have formed the basis of astrology up to modern times), among many others. Astrology was controversial even then, however. Just as today, certain scientists contested its value, claiming that a person's life could not be determined by their date of birth.

It was during this period that Hippocrates, the Greek physician known as the father of modern medicine, established a link between medicine and astrology, referring in particular to the link between physical organisms and the signs of the zodiac. According to his system, each sign governed a particular part of the body: for example, Aries, the head (the brain and sight); Taurus, the throat (the thyroid, the speech organs); Gemini, the upper rib cage and arms (the lungs, manual skills); and so on down the list, ending with Pisces, governing the feet.

The Chaldean astrological theory was circulated in Greece by the priest of Bal Berossos, who came from Babylon to settle on the island of Kos in 270 BC. The Greeks venerated him and leading contemporary astrologists and stoics included his theories in their system of philosophy. They decided it was *Pneuma*, the Greek wind, or spirit, which determined the course of events from the beginning of time, and that the movements of the planets were the visible signs of successions of this cause and effect.

A book (of which we have fragments) written in Egypt in around 150 BC and attributed to the scholars Nechepso and Petosiris established the practice of Greek astrology in a form that was subsequently to spread around the world. Astrologers of the time drew much inspiration from this highly respected textbook, and referred to it in their own works.

THE WORKS OF THE GREEK ASTRONOMER, PTOLEMY

Although many Egyptian texts were destroyed by the fire in the great library of Alexandria in around 48 AD, we nevertheless know that ancient Egypt, where religious matters pervaded everyday and political life, was subject to the influence of the Chaldean priests.

The Greco-Roman period saw the birth of the great Greek astronomer and mathematician, Ptolemy, in Alexandria (c. 90–168). In the famous library (where he is believed to have been the librarian) he defined the positions of approximately a thousand stars and constellations on the basis of previous works. He created the system that bears his name (Ptolemaic) and which places the Earth at the centre of the universe, with the planets revolving around it. This geocentric theory was to shape Western thought for over a millennium, until the ideas of Nicolas Copernicus became established in the 16th century. Ptolemy was the author of numerous books, including, notably, the *Tetrabiblos*, which was made accessible at the end of

SUN WORSHIP

The pharaoh Akhenaton (Amenophis IV), whose name means, 'He in whom Aton (the Sun God) is satisfied', and his wife Nefertiti offering the symbol of Maat (truth) to the Aton.

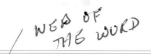

the first millennium thanks to Arabic translations (the original was lost) and which forms the basis of modern astrology. The first part of the book justifies the practice of astrology and offers a defence against its detractors. The second forms the basis of world astrology, and applies to particular countries. The third deals with individuals, and focuses on the moment of conception of a human being. Finally, the fourth is devoted to the progression of life. The serious imprecision of his work and the fact that he was familiar with the celestial phenomenon of the precession of the equinoxes and the heliocentric theory of the universe with the Sun at the centre yet did not take them into account, perhaps indicates that he may have been forced to hide his knowledge and even distort it for his personal safety.

IN AND OUT OF FAVOUR IN THE ROMAN EMPIRE

The Romans were divided on the subject of astrology. Some rejected it by putting forward logical arguments, and priests attempted to spurn the proclamations of astrologers. After the persecutions initially imposed on them, the Chaldean magi finally found favour with the emperors, and Augustus expressed his belief by having his star sign, Capricorn, engraved on coins. However, in *De Divinatione*, written in 44 BC, Cicero, who had supported astrology in his youth, tried to invalidate it. He argued that twins born in the same place could have very different destinies and that, conversely, men born at different times and in different places sometimes had the same destiny, ending their days on the same battlefield. Astrology finally did gain recognition under Tiberius and Nero, but when Nero died, Vespasian was unexpectedly proclaimed Emperor in 69 AD. He restored order after a troubled period of civil wars and rapidly gained the trust of the people, who saw in him indications of divine favour. Vespanian's reforms included attempting to abolish astrology, but it survived, re-establishing itself as a substitute for the lack of religious beliefs.

THE ARMILLARY SPHERE
Three-dimensional representation of the main structures of the cosmos. With the earth at its centre, the Ptolemaic system has long symbolised the general harmony of the world.

In 335–337 AD, the imperial lawyer, Firmicus Maternus Julius, wrote eight books on astrology, entitled *Mathematics, or the Power and Influence of the Stars*, which were to exert an enormous influence on astrologers up until the Renaissance. With the arrival of the Christian era in around the sixth century AD, astrologers disappeared throughout most of the Roman Empire, though they continued to flourish in the Middle East among the Jewish and Arabic nations.

ASTROLOGICAL TEACHINGS IN THE VEDA

Indian astrology is as old as that of the Sumerians. The Indus valley is one of the cradles of humanity and the source of sophisticated civilisations. From 1500 BC onwards, the *Veda*, the collection of Aryan hymns which were transmitted orally until written down in sacred books in the 6th century, retraced the history and rites of the gods and described the astrological knowledge and teachings which had been passed on by the priests.

Astronomy, medicine and astrology were based on a system underpinned by the revolutions of the Moon. The 27 Houses (*nakshatras*), used up until the third century BC, were associated with planets, symbols or divinities, each one of which corresponded approximately to the course followed by the Moon in a day. Each (*nakshatra*) linked with a star described specific characteristics and announced particular events. For example, *Anuradha*, the 17th house, symbolised by a lotus flower, was governed by Saturn and promised good health and vitality, and an ability to organise activities; it also encouraged travel and inspired jealousy, impulsive reactions and anger. When the predictions were unfavourable, it was customary to recite sacred formulae (*mantras*) and perform the rituals laid down in the Veda (particularly the *Rig-Veda*) in order to transform destiny and obtain the support of the divinities.

HINDU ASTROLOGY

Hindu astrology is based on the darshanam, a particular way of presenting reality, and allows for two possibilities: either destiny is revealed by personality, or vice versa.

When Alexandria was founded by Alexander the Great in 332, Greek culture spread east throughout the entire region as far as India. The Indians adopted the astrological techniques used by the Greeks, particularly the twelve signs of the zodiac, and used the same planets, Surya (the Sun), Soma (the Moon, a male god, as in Mesopotamia) and his wives. The latter were associated with the 27 houses. Indian astrology, which is basically quite similar to Western astrology, has developed freely over the centuries. Its difference lies in its use of a sidereal zodiac, which is linked to the stars rather than the seasons. The Hindus also observed the position of the lunar nodes (astronomical points linked to the Moon's orbit), a method that was, in turn, to be adopted by Western astrology. It was recognised and used by all castes in India and played its role in all the important parts of life, including marriage, business, medicine and religion. Its influence culminated in the works of Vahâra Mihira between the fourth and sixth centuries AD, which presented an overview of astronomical and astrological knowledge. The arrival of the Arabs in 632 AD led to further enriching exchanges between the two cultures. Indian astrology was still practised on a daily basis in this society, and the kings had their own personal astrologers. It remained intact up until the 18th century, when it underwent further changes due to British colonisation (though certain astrologers tried to maintain the tradition).

THE CHINESE ASTROLOGICAL SYSTEM

In the Far East, divination has been practised since the Neolithic period and developed alongside the Chinese cosmological system with its applications, particularly in medicine. Seers used the

shoulder-blades of cattle or the shells of tortoises (an animal reputed for its wisdom and long life and therefore able to offer guidance), which were hollowed out at a number of specific points. After asking one of the King's forebears a question, the seers placed a heated stick in one of the cavities. They were able to predict the future by interpreting the cracks or lines (*jiaguwen*, precursors of the *Yi Jing*, the Book of Transformations) produced by the effect of heat on the shell. The first traces of this practice found in northern China date back to the fourth millennium BC. Under the Shang dynasty (1766–1122 BC), seers offered their services to the King in order to determine political matters and the organisation of power, to predict the success of the forthcoming hunting season or to foresee whether the next eclipse would have a favourable or unfavourable effect. The questions to which the seers were requesting answers were carved onto the shell or bone, for example. Traces of carvings have been found that are so tiny that it would suggest the objective was to keep the questions secret. Over 100,000 such inscriptions have been discovered so far.

The *jiaguwen* attracted the attention of the Chinese authorities, who decided to carry out excavations in the last capital of the Shang dynasty, Anyang (in the province of Henan). The searches began in 1920 and continued up until the invasion of China by Japan in 1937. Over 150,000 items were found during this period. The practice of divination using shells or bones disappeared with the overthrow of the Shang dynasty by the Zhou dynasty which was to rule from 1122–255 BC. The *Yi Jing* (*The Book of Transformations*) became the new oracle, and was consulted by using stalks of the sacred plant, *achillea millefolium*, which were cast and arranged into groups of lines which could then be looked up in the book and an interpretation found for the present or future situation. This text, which contains great wisdom, is based on the interplay of yin (feminine, objective, receptive, solitary) and yang (masculine, subjective, outward, social) natures according to Chinese philosophy, which represent the balance of characteristics in an individual's personality.

The tradition of Asian divination was also preserved in Tibet, a region that was less disrupted by wars during these ancient times. The teachings of the mythical Chinese king, Fu Hi, who wrote a book on the art of divination and astrology, have also been found. According to legend, a monster with a horse's body and a dragon's head visited the country during his reign. The eight 'trigrams' (signs made up of three lines) that form the basis of the *Yi Jing* are said to have been inscribed on its back.

THE EMPEROR HUANGDI

By observing the sky and obtaining advice from his devotee, Qi Po, Emperor Huangdi defined the complete Chinese astrological system, which included the two qualities, yin and yang; the

THE EIGHT TRIGRAMS

*The trigrams, associated with the cardinal points, each symbolise a type of action,
an attitude, a character and an oracle.*

five elements (water, fire, metal, earth and wood) and the 12 signs (rat, ox, horse, dragon, etc). This marked the birth of Chinese astrology. He established the calendar, beginning in 2637 BC, created on the basis of monthly cycles determined by the moon and superposed annual cycles. It was so precise that it is still valid today. The horoscope, which was inextricably linked with all aspects of life, was used by the Chinese to help with ordinary or important decisions, setting auspicious dates for daily events, as well as for civil and religious ceremonies and for selecting a spouse.

In the third century BC, the Chinese philosopher, Zhou Yen, applied these theories to politics, asserting that the dynasties were governed by the elements (fire, earth, air and water) and that governments had to be in harmony with celestial laws – based on the advice of seers – if they were to maintain their power.

Chinese astrology no longer plays a role in deciding the fate of the nation, but continues to influence the lives of the people and interest in its system has spread to people all over the world. Like Western astrology, it divides the birth chart into 12 houses. However, it also makes use of 111 stars, including the planets known to Western astrology.

THE MAGIC CALENDAR OF THE MAYAS

On the other side of the world, in Central America, the Mayan civilisation established its own calendar, beginning in 3113 BC, which the Maya defined as the year in which the world was created. The Maya, who rose to prominence in around 300 AD, inherited the culture of the Olmec, a neighbouring people of more ancient origin who arose around 1200 BC. The Maya cleared the forests to build roads, cities and temples in a highly sophisticated and artistic architectural style. Their system of writing dates back to around 700 BC and consists of signs (glyphs), which correspond to words or syllables. Mayan cosmology was based on cycles of 5,200 years. The current cycle ends in 2012, whilst the current Chinese cycle – which began in 2637 BC in the sign of the Rat – is to end in 2020 when it will enter the sign of the Buffalo. These dates are very close and not far removed from the Western astrology's Age of Aquarius, which starts in around 2000 (an exact date for its beginning cannot be established). The Maya believed that at the centre of the cosmos was a great tree, its branches reaching into the heavens and its roots into the earth. Each of the four corners of the sky – and the four directions (north, south, east and west) – was represented by cosmic creatures such as a dog or a crocodile. According to *Popol Vuh*, the Maya Book of Genesis, the mythical heroic twins, Hunahpu and Xbalanque, restored world order by killing an evil bird which sat at the top of a

THE AZTEC CALENDAR

The Aztecs also developed an extremely complex calendar system, combining astronomical and metaphysical observations with the seasons and the movements of the stars.

tree. They were later harshly punished by the gods for playing their games too noisily, but survived their 'deaths', returning from Xibalba (the underworld) to be reborn as the Sun and Moon. This myth promised life after death, and Mayan temple imagery shows that the rulers Pacal (615–683 AD) and his son Chan Bahlum ('Serpent Jaguar', 684–702 AD) chose to have themselves depicted as taking on the personae of the twins. It was believed that they safeguarded world order and honoured their ancestors through rituals and games involving blood sacrifice, which took place within shrines representing both earthly and celestial monsters.

The Mayan priests used three calendars based on a mathematical system designed to harmonise actual time, the solar year and the revolutions of the various heavenly bodies. The first calendar was called *The Long Count*, and was used for looking back in time and recording events. There were also two cyclical calendars, a solar one called *Haab* which was used for practical and agricultural matters, and a sacred one called *Tzolkin*. These two were combined to form the Maya year of 360 days (18 months of 20 days), plus five nameless days of *uayed* (bad luck and danger) at the end of the year, on which no action of any importance (even cleaning the house) was undertaken. This system allowed the Maya to predict the future and set the dates for major events in advance, as each day was associated with omens, which were repeated periodically. The meeting of these two cyclical calendars created the Sacred Round of 52 years, a cycle sacred to all the ancient peoples of Mesoamerica and called 'the binding of the years'. It was thought that the end of this cycle could mark the end of the world if the gods were not satisfied with man's behaviour. The priests observed the movements of the Sun, the planets and the stars and had an extremely sophisticated understanding of astrology. Architects aligned temples, squares and tombs with the Sun (at the equinoxes) or with the stars. They worshipped the planet Venus (also identified with the god Quetzalcoatl) in particular, believing that as the morning star it pulled the Sun up into the sky and from it they could predict the future. They foresaw eclipses, and activities and phenomena in the skies were seen as episodes in the lives of the gods. Religion, astrology and the calendar formed an inseparable whole, which helped to ensure the smooth running of society.

THE ARABIC INFLUENCE

Arab astrologers and astronomers had a great influence on cultural life in Europe between the 9th and 15th centuries.

In spite of the decline of their civilisation and the devastating effect of the Spanish conquest in the early 16th century, priests in Central America continued to use the sacred calendar for their magical, religious and astrological activities and it has been re-discovered and studied throughout the world in recent years.

THE PROGRESS OF ARAB AND JEWISH ASTROLOGER/SCIENTISTS

The position of astrologers in the Middle East at the beginning of the Christian era was completely different. For the first Christians, astrology was a heresy and astrologers were considered charlatans and subsequently lost all influence. In 321, Emperor Constantine, who had converted to the new Christian religion, banned astrology and sentenced anyone practising it to death. Astrology thus disappeared for centuries, taking knowledge of astronomy with it. Even though the founders of the Church tried to make a distinction between the astronomical sciences and astrology, this resulted in the Christian countries lagging behind considerably in scientific terms.

During the same period, Arabic and Jewish people who had settled in Western Europe after the conquest of Spain by the Moors began to exert their influence. The Jews had recorded their knowledge of the past in their holy books, the precious *Talmud*, the *Zohar* and the *Sepher Yetzirah* (*The Book of Creation*). The two latter works are filled with astrological calculations and interpretations. The *Cabbala*, which describes the workings of the spiritual hierarchies of the universe and creation on the basis of the Tree of Life, and the *Sephiroth* (the existence of God as revealed by the planets), is closely linked to astrology. The Jews made a distinction between astronomy and astrology, but recognised both.

The Arabs, notably the Caliph Al-Mansour (the founder of Bagdad) and his son Haroun Al-Rashid, introduced the science of astrology into their empire. They studied mathematics and astronomy and invited Jewish scholars to their palace. In 777, the scientist Jacob ben Tarik founded a school for astrology and astronomy which became a leading intellectual centre. For the Arabs, astrology was inseparable from astronomy, which was considered to be its practical application. The works of the leading scientists and astrologers Abu Mashar, Shabbethai Donalo and Abraham ibn Ezrah, were recognised and studied throughout the

THE ASTROLOGER
Looking up at the stars, the astrologer probes the immensity of space and time to try to find man's place in the firmament.

Middle Ages in Europe. They also referred to the works of Ptolemy, which they developed and translated, and in some cases supplemented with deterministic interpretations stemming from Jewish beliefs.

NOSTRADAMUS, COPERNICUS AND KEPLER

Until the influence of Arabic studies became established at the time of the Crusades, the only form of astrology remaining in the West was that linked to agriculture and peasant activities. (As can be seen in the *Book of Hours* painted for the Duc de Berry in France in 1410, in which the

changing occupations of the months are portrayed along with astrological imagery relating to the specific time of year). However, the Jews also made astrology more widespread through their religious and astronomical teachings and gradually astrologers were to resume their role of counsellors in royal courts.

Astrology began to develop further during the Renaissance and, in Italy, governments (and even popes) managed their affairs on the basis of advice from astrologers. Scientists and university scholars also often took an interest in the subject. The founder of modern astrology, German astronomer Johannes Kepler (who established the laws describing the orbits of the planets) earned his living by creating horoscopes, and it was said that he was extremely skilful at predicting future events.

In France, Catherine de Medici had an astrological observatory built and called upon the services of Nostradamus (1503–1566). A French astrologer and physician, Michel de Nostre Dame came from a rich family of traders and could have led a prosperous quiet life had he not secretly maintained contact with his rather unusual great grandfather. The latter, a rebellious, free-thinking doctor who had been banned from the profession for illegally manufacturing medicines, passed on his mathematical and astrological knowledge to his grandson. Under his influence, Nostradamus became a doctor, alchemist, astrologer and seer and devised his prescriptions on the basis of astrology. He predicted the weather, concocted medicines and plant-based remedies for the plague (which he successfully tried out during an epidemic in Aix-en-Provence) and wrote his famous prophesies in the form of rhyming quatrains (*Centuries astrologiques* in 1555). Many of his predictions came true during his lifetime, particularly those concerning politics, such as the death of Henri II and the reign of Henri IV. He even foresaw his own death – succumbing to gout in 1566, as he had predicted.

THE 19TH CENTURY

Thanks to Romanticism, astrology became the subject of much research, combining philosophy, religion and psychology.

Polish astronomer Nicolaus Copernicus established the theory of the heliocentric system (the dual movement of the planets on their own axes and around the Sun), which was welcomed by astrologers. He did not publish his work until a few days before his death in 1543, as he feared the reaction of theologians. His theory, according to which the Earth was not in the centre of the universe, was to form the basis of the scientific revolution of the 17th century. Italian physicist and astronomer Galileo Galilei (1564–1642) and Johannes Kepler (1571–1630) were to the supply the proof that was needed to underpin the system propounded by Copernicus. From the 17th century onwards, the rapid development of scientific thought created a separation between astronomy and astrology. In 1665, French statesman Colbert

banned the teaching of astrology in French universities. From then on, its importance declined to make way for the spirit of the Enlightenment, which developed a scientific approach to reality and gradually took over from the religious vision. Astrology was then relegated to the position of a folk custom.

However, in England and the United States, esoteric orders such as the Rosicrucians (who were concerned with wisdom derived from ancient mystical doctrines) and the Freemasons prospered. At the beginning of the 18th century, American astrologers were quietly continuing their studies and certain universities, notably Yale and Harvard, cautiously began to acknowledge astrology, which was also being studied in Masonic lodges. Leading figures such as Benjamin Franklin (who published an astrological almanac in 1733, under the pseudonym of R. Saunders), Thomas Jefferson and George Washington expressed an interest in these ideas and referred to them throughout their lives. By the beginning of the 19th century, astrological data, books and dictionaries were being published on a regular basis.

A BURGEONING MOVEMENT ONCE MORE

Astrology re-emerged in force in the 19th century, with the increased recognition of occultism in response to the excessive rationalism of the time. The psychic sciences increased in popularity, with the use of ouija boards, for those seeking contact with the dead. Writers and artists also showed an interest (Victor Hugo and Conan Doyle were interested in Spiritualism, and Irish poet W. B. Yeats studied astrology). Theosophists, who sought to know God by a form of mystical intuition, began to pay attention to astrology, and it was thanks to the Englishman, Alan Leo (1869–1917), one of the founding fathers of The Astrological Lodge of Great Britain, that its popularity returned in the UK.

On the eve of the 20th century, the Golden Dawn groups such as the Rosicrucians (founded by Max Heindel) and the Anthroposophists (created by Rudolf Steiner), who were concerned with esoteric wisdom derived from ancient mystical doctrines, practised astrology on a regular basis and gained new respect for the subject, reviving Eastern religions and philosophies and the Cabbala (the sacred Jewish book). People again began to look to the past to draw meaning from their lives, and new research movements were created. Modern science rejected this trend, though specialists in the emerging subject of psychology considered it with interest, particularly in connection with the work of Carl Gustave Jung.

In the USA in the early 1930s, Dane Rudhyar, a philosopher, composer and astrologer, was the original writer of the *American Astrology* horoscope. He studied the influence of the Moon and its phases on human behaviour. His astrological work focused on people as a whole, rather than simply in terms of the events affecting them. His work turned astrology into a practical tool, which could be used for personal development. Humanist astrology, which focuses on the individual's life and development, originates from this school.

A number of other researchers were working along different lines at the same time. In France, attempts were being made to justify astrology by the analysis of statistical data. After the Second World War, Paul Choisnard, a graduate of the *École Polytechnique*, and Michel Gauquelin (who was intending to discredit rather than support astrology), analysed the frequency of the positions of certain planets in the birth chart according to the activities of the person born under them. Mars for sportsmen, for example, and Saturn for politicians and scientists. Though their results were impressive, they still did not convince the sceptics. Astrologers realised that they needed to develop knowledge of their science in order to dispel the aura of superstition surrounding it. In their search for increased credibility, they examined different fields, including psychoanalysis and medicine. Astrologers also argued that there might be still unknown planets (the most recent one, Pluto, was only discovered in 1930) and fascination with this new popular science grew steadily among the experts.

A FRACTURED SOCIETY IN SEARCH OF MEANING

These studies and debates on astrology eventually sparked wide interest among the general public. The trauma of the Second World War had left the world in shock and obsessed by the nuclear threat. For the first time, mankind had the means for mass self-destruction. Nazism had shown that people could behave with a terrifying, deliberate cruelty unmatched by any other living species. Massacres, genocides, interminable

THE FUTURE OF THE WORLD

The branch of astrology that predicts events is practised by numerous traditional astrologers.

wars and destructive totalitarian regimes had inflicted suffering on some part of the world throughout the centuries, but it was not until the last century and the era of mass communication that ordinary people became fully aware of what was happening globally. In Western society, the gap between the haves and the have-nots widened. Technological advances happened at such a rate that people were left bewildered in a world that seemed a very different place from the one they were born into.

For many people, religions, sciences and political and social ideologies fail to provide answers to the 'big' questions of modern-day life, and indeed, are sometimes even held partly responsible for the world's tragedies. People therefore turn to astrology, on a personal and broader level, to try and

make sense of the world. It is entertaining to read one's horoscope in the daily paper, even if it is immediately forgotten, but this fleeting contact with the irrational gives people a chance to believe that things can change for the better. If the horoscope is good, it is seen as a promise of happiness; if it is less encouraging, its effects will only be temporary and tomorrow's may be more hopeful. Others consult astrologers very seriously, with the object of analysing their destinies. For them it can be a way of regaining control over their lives. On a very practical level, astrology provides explanations and advice on relationships, professional projects and personal life.

GROWING MEDIA INTEREST

Astrology became fashionable between 1960 and 1970 in the context of the hippie movement and psychedelic culture, with its emphasis on expanding the mind's awareness on many different levels and its ideals and dreams of universal peace and love. Western society at this time was in the process of being transformed by youth culture. As television made its way into every home and magazines flourished, astrology became increasingly more popular, with astrologers becoming established as media personalities and attracting faithful followers. The best of them succeeded in combining – even in a brief daily, weekly or monthly Sun sign horoscope – a sense of sound astrological knowledge of planetary movements and influences with skillfully-written philosophical advice on love and relationships, work and health. By the time of his death in the mid-1990s, the English astrologer, Patrick Walker had his work syndicated throughout the world in various magazines and journals, and had acquired the status almost of a magus. Perhaps as proof of this, there was great speculation immediately after his death as to who would take his place as the pre-eminent astrologer, and he was posthumously attacked as a 'charlatan' by one outraged critic of astrology.

During the 1970s, many astrologers became established in the United States, where they created schools and research movements, exchanging their knowledge and producing advanced and wide-ranging research. As a result, astrology began to become more valued and respected. At the same time, in England and Germany, serious astrologers were also studying and developing the field.

ASTROLOGICAL CALCULATION SOFTWARE

Nowadays software for astrological calculation displays the birth chart in a fraction of a second, in sharp contrast to the interminable measurements that had to be made by practitioners until very recently.

THE COMPLEX TECHNOLOGY OF ASTROLOGY

The first computer software for use in astrological calculation and interpretation was created in the 1960s, and the use of computers became more widespread between 1980 and 1990, enabling astrologers to devote their energy to interpretation and research rather than

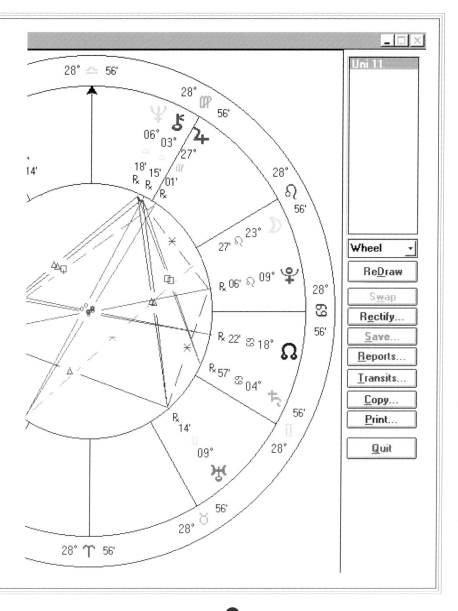

Wheel

ReDraw

Swap

Rectify...

Save...

Reports...

Transits...

Copy...

Print...

Quit

fastidious calculations. A wide range of software became available at varying prices – accessible as packages to buy through shops or the Internet (details of some of the most useful programmes and astrology software websites are given in Find Out). Telephone services – offering a personalised 'reading' for a fee – also began to spring up, creating confusion between astrology and fortune-telling and making it easier for practitioners with little or no training to become established. These practitioners often use other supports, such as tarot cards or direct intuition (claiming they can access special knowledge of a person simply through 'feeling'), which can be accessed much more quickly and easily than detailed astrological calculation. Unfortunately, some practitioners are either not genuine or not very adept at their craft and sometimes exploit the credulity of their clients. Generally, however, dedicated astrologers strive to use their art to help others on an honest basis and sometimes under difficult conditions. Astrologers must undergo rigorous training and testing to become certified, and the subject demands a great deal of commitment and would be impossible without personal dedication. However, the range and quality of astrological readings is continuing to develop, from the anodyne daily horoscope (often technically inaccurate) to guidance astrology and the sophisticated scientific theories of sociologists or historians such as Lester Ness in the United States, who conduct documented scientific research.

CONSULTING THE STARS IN THE EAST

In India, consulting the astrologer forms an integral part of daily life (irrespective of the caste of the individual). People consult him for advice on both public and private matters.

A MARGINAL PRACTICE

Astrology has often been considered a marginal practice, reserved for unorthodox people. However, in reality it has long been used by people in positions of power and influence, from world leaders like President Reagan (whose wife consulted astrologers on his behalf) to royalty (Princess Diana), business leaders such as J. P. Morgan (who allegedly used astrology to amass his fortune at the end of the 19th century) and many familiar names from show business (perhaps reflecting the uncertainty of their profession).

The question of whether certain professions tend to encourage people to belive more in astrology is an interesting one. A study by sociologists, for example, perhaps surprisingly revealed that middle and senior executives tend to believe more in astrology than other social groups. An increasing numbers of scientists (notably the astrophysicist, Hubert Reeves) are considering astrology from a neutral, or even favourable, standpoint.

In Eastern cultures, astrology has never disappeared from daily or official life. Birth charts are still drawn up for newborn babies, providing future guidance for them over, for example, the choice of marriage partner. Private and public events are planned after consulting the birth chart and astrology is still used by doctors for the purpose of diagnosis, as it was in the past. In certain cultures – most notably India and China – it has remained an essential part of daily life. In the Western world, Christianity regards astrology as being at odds with the teachings of the Bible, though for some people, astrology fills the void created by the decline in religious belief (sociologists have noted that its development is inversely proportional to the practice of religion). But astrology can also be seen as part of a more holistic view of life, in which an individual can achieve a broader understanding of their existence, reconciling all its dimensions, including the spiritual, and seeking a balance between sensitivity and intuition, good sense and practicality.

THE MYSTICAL ELEMENT

After breaking away from Western forms of religion, astrology embraced a new type of mystical understanding in which personal, internal experience could be assimilated and combined with a sense of the universal. Through astrological analysis, in which the human being is thought to be constituted of four modes (physical, emotional, mental and spiritual), which were also expressed in the birth chart, a multi-dimensional vision can be obtained. In this way, astrology can help individuals to discover and understand their personality as a whole, whilst more conventional forms of analysis tend to offer only partial, disconnected solutions to life's problems.

NEW AGE

In this image produced at the end of the 20th century, Jesus, after the resurrection, appears to the two pilgrims of Emmaus and is confronted by that symbol of modernity, the computer.

Groups and associations concerning astrology now exist in every country. They publish reviews, create databases of astrological information, provide directories of practitioners, offer advice, organise conferences and manage Internet sites. Key people associated with these, such as Alexander Ruperti, Stephen Arroyo and Liz Greene, have received international recognition. Their approaches may differ but they are usually linked, the research based on common knowledge built up over the years just as it is in the scientific world.

The modern manifestation of the 19th-century practice, *channelling* has been developing simultaneously since the 1960s. When channelling occurs, messages – sometimes entire books – are communicated directly into the mind of the person receiving the information (the medium), as if by some form of intuitive process. The information is thought to come from another world (either from non-incarnate spirits, or the medium's own subconscious), and the purpose is to help humanity in general and open up to new forms of consciousness.

THE MATHEMATICAL PRECISION OF ASTROLOGY

Over recent years, numerous alternative therapies and methods for achieving greater self-awareness or predictive ability have developed, varying in seriousness and reliability. Astrology is sometimes mistakenly grouped with these practices but is, in fact, very different, as it is based on an extremely precise, mathematical system of calculations which must be carried out according to precise rules.

Astrology involves the close study of specific groups of elements – the signs of the zodiac (representing the qualities and characteristics); the planets in the solar system (representing the psychological functions – willpower, emotion, feelings, thoughts, etc) and the Houses of the birth chart (or sectors, representing different areas of life such as work or family). These three groups of elements interact and are measured and interpreted according to precise, codified laws (known as positions, aspects and lordship). The birth chart follows the same basic plan and using rigorously transcribed astronomical data, it constitutes the map of the actual positions of physical bodies and geometric reference points in space. This must then be interpreted by the astrologer according to the individual personality and data, which will, of course, vary. The procedures followed in astrology are based on clearly defined principles and follow logical reasoning. Accuracy as to timing is hugely important in the drawing up of the birth chart, as this will affect the positions and aspects and therefore the influences on an individual's personality.

THE SKIES – A MIRROR IMAGE

The basic assumption of astrology is similar to that of an analogy, or the idea that what happens here on Earth is a reflection of what is above us (in the sky). Carl Gustave Jung referred to this as 'synchonicity', or in other words, meaningful coincidences. Thus, the planets do not make things happen or influence things on earth, they merely mirror it. There can be no gravitational nor electromagnetic influence being exerted by the planets, because if it were, the effects would be detectable in some way and therefore measurable. Astrology's great value in terms of human psychology is that it enables people to understand themselves and the world around them better and therefore to cope with life's difficulties.

THE PIC DU MIDI OBSERVATORY, FRANCE

The movement of the stars caused by the rotation of the Earth on its own axis can be captured in a photograph using a long exposure time.

Because the sky is reflecting what happens on Earth, by observing the sky it is possible to gain a deeper understanding of what is happening on Earth. The sky reflects the Earth, or rather the Earth reflects the sky, or both, in a kind of mirror effect. When Jung studied the links between psychology and alchemy, he developed the theory that things happen in a parallel, synchronised manner on different levels, without there being any cause-and-effect relationship between them. It is apparent that the universe is filled with synchronicity, regardless of scientific claims. This symmetry is so subtle that it is possible to describe a person's characteristics on one level (his life) on the basis of another (his astral configurations). The study can be pursued to such a degree that the analysis of these characteristics or inclinations becomes almost exact. The birth chart shows the direction a person's life can take. This is often described as being like someone negotiating a river. As he or she sails down it, they will encounter many things that can affect their course; the steepness of the banks or the smooth beaches bordering it; the rocks and the rapids that harbour danger; the tranquil pools that can be sailed through easily; the storms which might disrupt the journey; friends on the banks or assailants in ambush. It is up to the individual person – to decide how to respond to whatever they encounter on the way. They are free to choose whether to drift along with the current or try to return upstream; fighting against the elements or using them to their advantage. The more familiar a person is with their particular river, the easier their choices will be. The birth chart therefore provides a guide. Astrology cannot predict a person's reactions, as that is up to them. The role of astrology is to assess the situation at the outset or over time and to give an idea of the advantages and options which may be available to the person, but it is up to the individual to decide whether or not to use them and in what way.

THE AGE OF AQUARIUS

We are leaving the mystical Age of Pisces to enter the more technical, spiritual Age of Aquarius. What does the future hold for mankind?

This is why astrology fails when it is too predictive and inflexible. It fulfils its function best by encouraging responsibility and freedom to act. The concept of astrology indicates that the world is not simply based on logic and materialism. We know that it is also irrational, magical, emotional and aesthetic. The idea of synchronicity can be applied to disciplines other than astrology and forms the basis of all known divinatory and predictive approaches. Even advanced science gives some evidence of this (quantum mechanics, for example, allows the possibility for a similar theory of synchronicity), and perhaps in the future science may help to unravel a greater understanding of how astrology works.

Taking a different approach, the English biologist, Rupert Sheldrake, defined what he called a 'morphic' or 'morphogenetic' field, referring to an unknown field of nature, which could be linked to any animate or inanimate object and which would define its form, structure and activities. Any new objects found to be similar to the latter would also be affected by this field, which would try to model them in its image, enabling unconscious communication between organisms. This would explain why, for example, scientists make the same discovery independently at the same time in different parts of the world; why new types of behaviour develop at the same time in

different environments; and why the universe is organised in a series of repeated structures (in atoms, stellar systems, galaxies). The astrological system works in a similar way.

THE NEW MILLENNIUM

At the beginning of the new millennium, astrology appears to be in a fairly strong position. It has gathered strength from the sheer number of people who adhere to it, to a greater or lesser degree, to help them lead their lives.

It still has its attackers, but they are unable to find arguments capable of discouraging its supporters. Meanwhile, researchers are looking for new directions and applications with which to broaden the scope of astrology and link it to other disciplines. Astrology is governed by the planet Uranus, which symbolises accomplished humanity, creativity, freedom and consciousness as well as technical progress and unlimited communication. It can be used to interpret a wide range of experience – there are very few areas of life it does not cover.

The Age of Aquarius will succeed that of Pisces for a period of around 2,000 years. It is not possible to say exactly when it will begin, but most calculations make it around 2000. Historically, the Age of Pisces coincided with the era of Christianity, and was marked by the characteristics of the sign, self-sacrifice and the search for a balance between spiritual aspirations and survival needs. The Age of Aquarius is thought to mark the start of a period of knowledge and progress, fraternity between peoples (not only on Earth but throughout the universe as a whole), individual fulfilment and a respect for the ecological balance of the Earth. Having freed itself to a large extent from its aura of magic and superstition, astrology is now recognised by practitioners of human sciences as a tool for gaining self-knowledge and a long-term vision of situations. With devotees around the world, its popularity and longevity seem assured. Perhaps if we can open our minds sufficiently, it will eventually help us to gain a greater understanding of the mysteries of the universe.

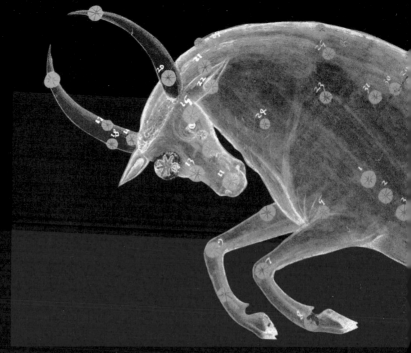

PICTORIAL REPRESENTATIONS OF THE DIFFERENT SIGNS OF THE ZODIAC AND
THE PART OF THE YEAR THEY RELATE TO.
THE ZODIAC IS THE BAND OF SKY IN WHICH THE PLANETS MOVE.
THE MESOPOTAMIANS DIVIDED IT INTO TWELVE SIGNS:
ARIES, TAURUS, GEMINI, CANCER, LEO, VIRGO, LIBRA, SCORPIO,
SAGITTARIUS, CAPRICORN, AQUARIUS AND PISCES.

Aries: 21 March–20 April

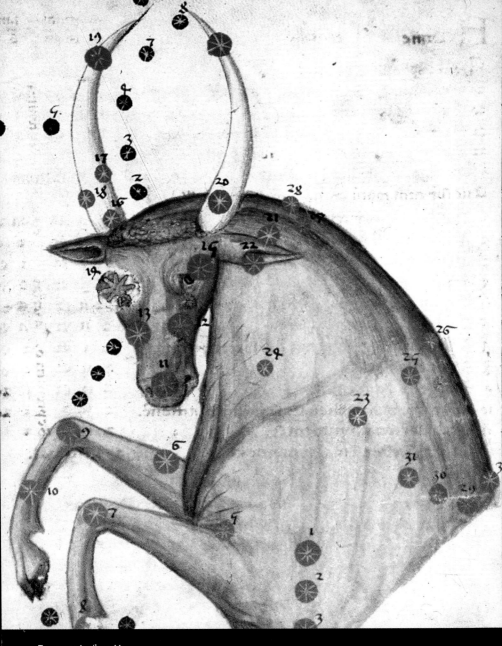

Taurus: 21 April–20 May

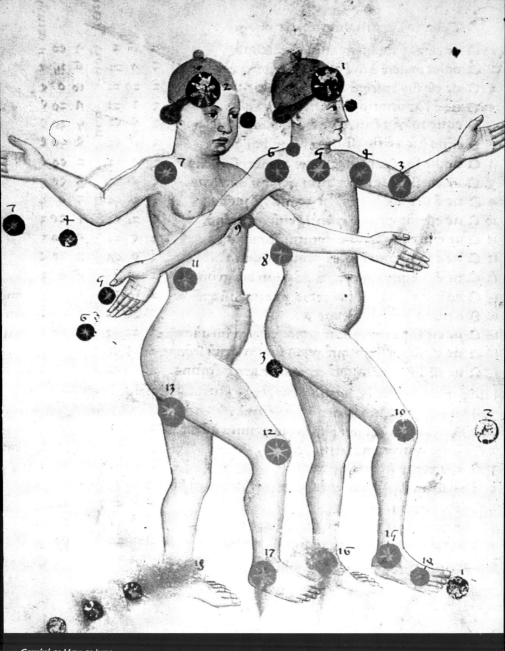

Gemini: *21 May–21 June*

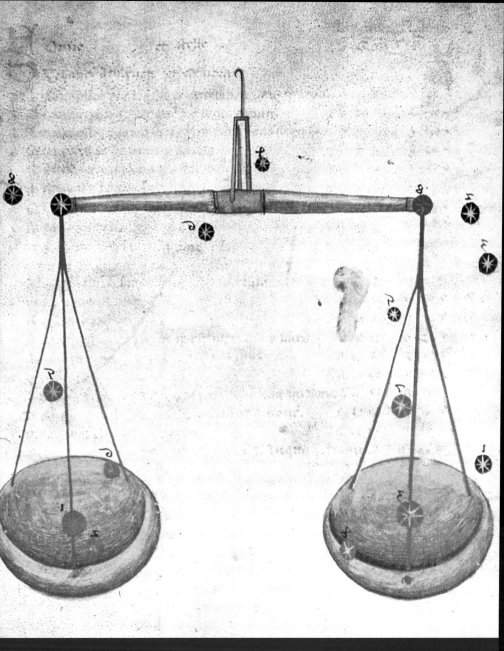

Libra: 23 September–22 October

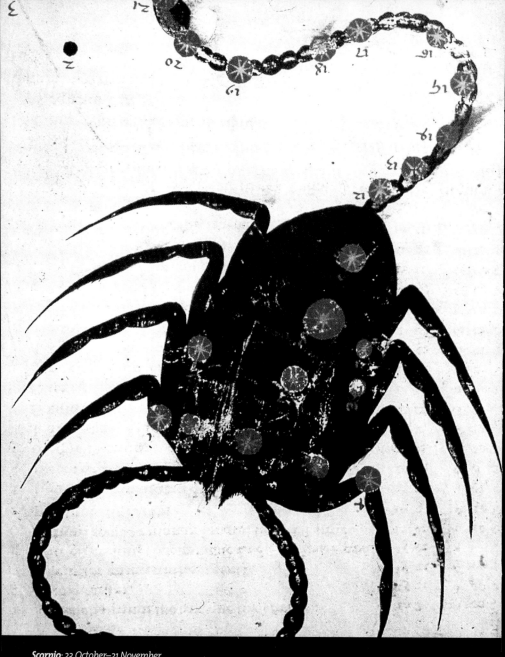

Scorpio: 23 October–21 November

Sagittarius: 22 November–20 December

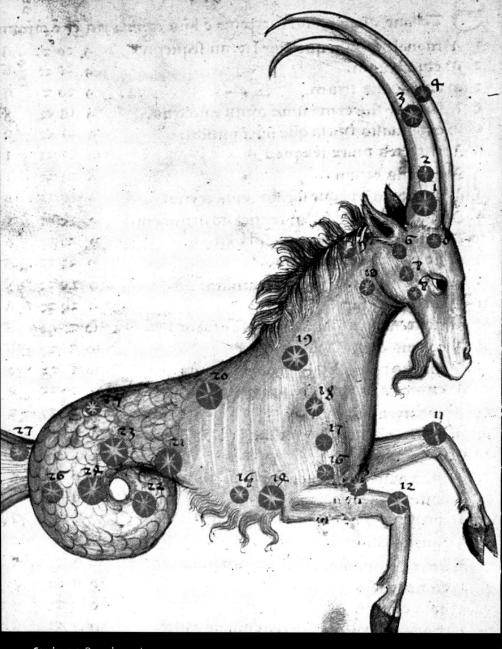

Capricorn: 21 December–19 January

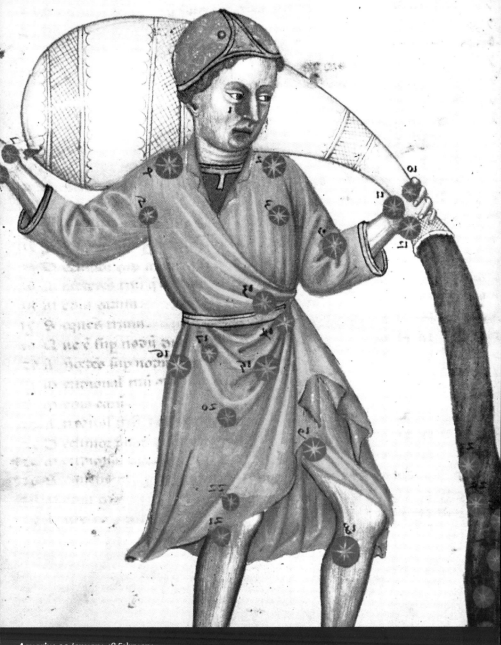

Aquarius: 20 January–18 February

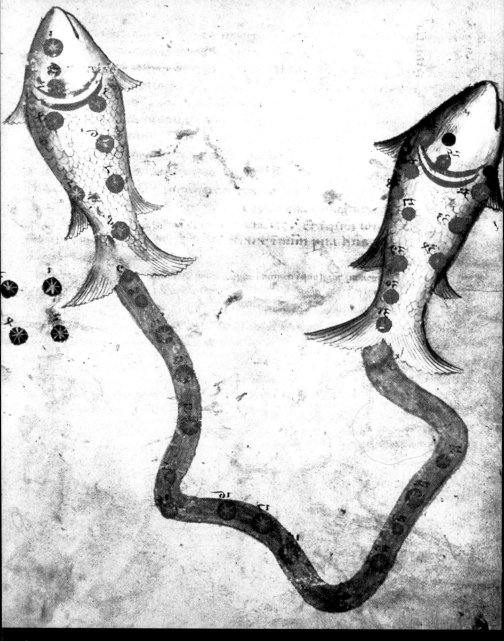

Pisces: *19 February–20 March*

IN PRACTICE

The birth chart

The birth chart is the map of the sky at the time of a person's birth. It represents the projection of the planets on the 'ecliptic' (a circular plan showing the Sun's yearly path). The birth chart represents the basic qualities and potential of an individual and can be referred to throughout their life. If we take a geocentric point of view (from the Earth) the subject of the chart is placed at the centre of the diagram on the Earth. The heliocentric approach (with the Sun is at the centre) is sometimes suggested as the correct view since it reflects how the solar system works. However, it is used less frequently as it does not show the influences converging on the Earth and therefore it does not apply to a person's everyday experience.

The time of birth

At the time of birth, the Sun is positioned in one of the four quadrants that divide the day (6am–noon, for example), and in the sign of the zodiac relating to that time. The date therefore defines the Sun sign (or 'star' sign) and the time of the ascendant sign. Together they form a decisive combination, since the ascendant determines the way in which the solar sign is expressed. Each quadrant is divided into three Houses, each of which correspond to a specific area of activity.

The ascendant

The ascendant is the sign present on the horizon in the East at the time of birth and is calculated according to the local time of birth. It explains how a person finds their place on earth and describes their relationship with the environment. The descendant, (the sign on the horizon in the West) symbolises relationships with others. The horizon line separates space into two semi-circles, with the centre of the sky (power) at the top and the depths of the sky (the origin of a being) at the base.

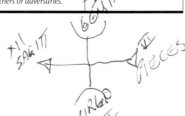

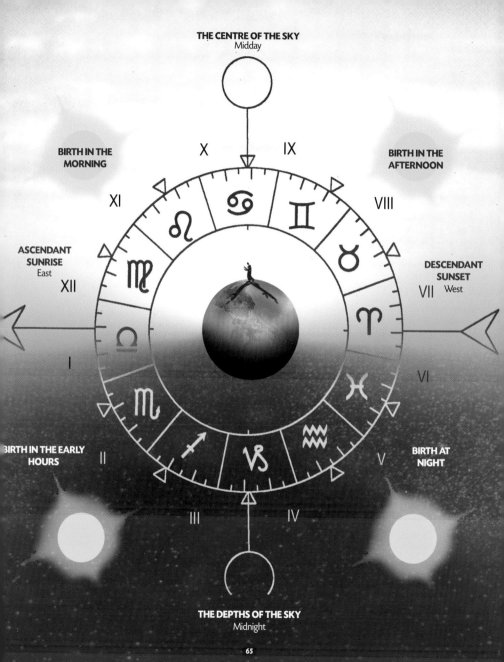

THE CENTRE OF THE SKY
Midday

BIRTH IN THE
MORNING

X   IX

BIRTH IN THE
AFTERNOON

XI   VIII

ASCENDANT
SUNRISE
East

XII

DESCENDANT
SUNSET
West

VII

I   VI

BIRTH IN THE EARLY
HOURS

II   V

BIRTH AT
NIGHT

III   IV

THE DEPTHS OF THE SKY
Midnight

The annual cycle of the Sun and the planets

The geocentric view (from the Earth), lists ten main planets (plus the Earth): the Sun and Moon, the 'luminaries'; Mercury and Venus, the internal planets (within our orbit); Mars, Jupiter and Saturn, the visible external planets; Uranus, Neptune and Pluto; and the 'distant' planets, which cannot be seen with the naked eye. Each planetary function is influenced by the sign of the zodiac it occupies.

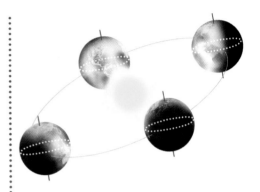

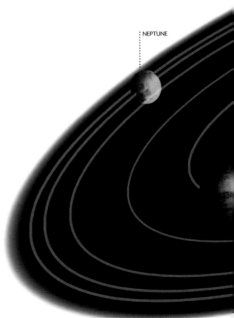

NEPTUNE

JUPITER

The Sun
The centre of energy. It radiates light and heat and its rays beat down on the Earth. It symbolises the ego, the conscious personality, willpower, supreme (possibly royal) power and masculine aspects.

The Moon
Orbit : 27 days.
It keeps watch over the night like a silver mirror. It symbolises sensitivity, the unconscious, the emotions, receptivity or passivity, maternal and feminine aspects.

Mercury
Orbit: 88 days.
This is the fastest-moving planet, lively, and always close to the Sun. It symbolises nervousness, intelligence, skills, thought, intellect, the nervous system, social exchanges and contacts.

Venus
Orbit: 225 days.
It revolves upside down, surrounded by clouds. It symbolises the emotions, aesthetics, the search for harmony and adaptability, the feminine aspects of beauty, peace and love.

Mars
Orbit: nearly two years. The dry, red planet. It symbolises a virile fighting spirit, strength, action and conquest.

Jupiter
Orbit: 12 years. A large planet characterised by its red spot, it radiates strong energy. It symbolises fulfilment and expansion, success, conviviality and generosity.

Saturn
Orbit: 29½ years. A planet surrounded by rings. It symbolises asceticism, willpower, concentration, structure, solitude and depth.

Uranus
Orbit: 84 years. A planet whose axis of rotation lies in the plane of its orbit. It symbolises individuality, creativity, originality, electrical or electromagnetic energy and technical aspects.

Neptune
Orbit: 165 years. Gaseous and remote, this planet symbolises artistic inspiration, sympathy, spiritual love, psychic powers, dreams and mysticism.

Pluto
Orbit: 248 years. This small, very distant planet symbolises transformations, destruction and regeneration, internal alchemy and nuclear energy.

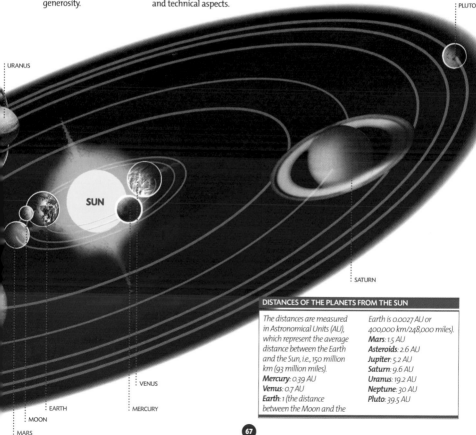

PLUTO

URANUS

SUN

SATURN

VENUS

EARTH

MOON

MARS

MERCURY

DISTANCES OF THE PLANETS FROM THE SUN

The distances are measured in Astronomical Units (AU), which represent the average distance between the Earth and the Sun, i.e., 150 million km (93 million miles).
Mercury: 0.39 AU
Venus: 0.7 AU
Earth: 1 (the distance between the Moon and the

Earth is 0.0027 AU or 400,000 km/248,000 miles).
Mars: 1.5 AU
Asteroids: 2.6 AU
Jupiter: 5.2 AU
Saturn: 9.6 AU
Uranus: 19.2 AU
Neptune: 30 AU
Pluto: 39.5 AU

The zodiac and the aspects

The zodiac, the 'circle of animals', is the band, or circular crown, in the sky in which the movements of the planets can be observed. Since Mesopotamian times, it has been divided into twelve equal parts of 30° each – twelve 'signs', which are symbolised by animals or characters. Each one is associated with a number of characteristics, qualities and behaviours. In Western astrology, the signs (linked to the natural cycle of the seasons) are defined on the basis of the vernal point (0° from Aries), which corresponds to the spring equinox.

The birth chart is interpreted on the basis of the different planetary positions, their interactions and the exchanges between defined points. Each planet is associated with one or two signs which it governs: for example, Mars is associated with Aries and Scorpio; Venus with Taurus and Libra; the Moon with Cancer; the Sun with Leo, Jupiter with Sagittarius and Pisces; Saturn with Capricorn and Aquarius; Uranus with Aquarius; Neptune with Pisces and Pluto with Scorpio.

THE TWELVE SIGNS

Arians have a determined, active, decisive, masculine character. They are leaders.

Taureans are receptive, patient, constructive and feminine. They are creators.

Geminians are open to discovery, meetings and exchanges. They are messengers.

Cancerians are sensitive, emotional, protective and dreamy. They are mother figures.

Leos are creative, proud, radiant, powerful and warm. They are father figures.

Virgos like to organise, verify, adapt and protect themselves. They are in control.

Librans define themselves by their relationships with others. They are partners.

Scorpios are whole and extreme; they live intense, passionate lives and communicate with invisible forces.

Sagittarians are fiery and fulfil their potential in the world they explore.

Capricorns are reflective and pursue their ambitious, secret aims. They are master figures.

Aquarians share and participate in what is universal. They are humanists.

Pisceans are mystics and poets and are driven by a search for unity.

The aspects

The aspects are the positions of the planets in relation to each other. Planets in aspect to each other are related by geometric angles, represented by transversal lines within the zodiacal crown and are expressed in degrees of longitude (which measure the angle of the arc of the circle between two given stars). By linking certain Houses and signs, the aspects – which are also known as angular intervals – reveal many different combinations in the action of the planets and describe harmonious relationships or internal conflicts between a person's different polarities. In other words, this can be advantageous to the person, or challenging. The main aspects are: conjunction, opposition, the square, the trine and the sextile. The others are classified as minor or secondary. The conjunction (0°) combines the energies of the two planets without affecting their ability to cooperate. The trine (120°) and the sextile (60°) offer reciprocal support to the planets. The square reveals tension or conflicts between them and the opposition highlights swings or alternations. The semi-sextile (30°) is an attenuated sextile; the semi-square (45°) and the sesqui-square (130°) both energise the planets; the quincunx (150°) presents an obstacle to be overcome; and the quintile (72°), a radiant, creative aspect.

Indira Gandhi

The birth chart of Indira Gandhi – a Scorpio with Leo ascendant, with Jupiter dominating and occupied by Capricorn – reveals her aptitude for power and attraction to politics. The Sun in House IV (that of the father and the homeland) shows that she inherited her political mission from her father, Jawaharlal Nehru. The obvious tensions in her chart indicate difficulties in her public, personal and emotional life. The imprisonment and deaths of both her husband, Feroze Gandhi, and her son, Sanjay, and finally her own assassination, are indicated by the opposition between Pluto and Venus. Mars in House I (the personality) explains her will to fight with conviction and reveals her efficiency and sense of organisation. However, her strengths, combined with her errors of judgement, a lack of diplomacy and long-term vision (evoked by the squares of Jupiter and Mercury and the opposition between Neptune and the Moon) provoked hostile reactions, even amongst her close contacts. This culminated in her assassination by her own guards during a religious ceremony – a context suggested by the positions of Jupiter and Neptune in her chart.

Mozart

Mozart was an Aquarian, with the ascendant in Virgo. His chart shows that his Sun is in House V, which symbolises artistic creation. Neptune, the planet of music, is in opposition with the Sun, which enhances the musical aspect and enables it to be expressed. Aquarius is a sign of universality, meetings and communication based on intuition, which encourages a tendency towards the avant-garde. In the conjunction of Saturn and the Sun, Mozart's creative aspect is combined with an ability to create timeless masterpieces unaffected by the vagaries of fashion (emphasised by the Sun in Aquarius). His compositions were inspired, in an almost mystical way, and he possessed powerful internal resources for creativity and imagination, some of which were hereditary (the Moon/Pluto in House IV). However, the same Sun-Saturn conjunction between the Sun and Saturn, also creates difficulties and delays success, which made his material life hazardous and demanding.

The orbit and the phases of the Moon

The Moon, the Earth's satellite, sets the rhythm of its days and nights and plays an essential role in the birth chart, as it does in nature in general.

ROTATIONS

The moon waxes from the New Moon to the Full Moon and then wanes from the Full Moon to the next New Moon as it moves from right to left.

The lunar months

The moon accompanies the Earth in its annual revolution around the Sun (approximately 13 annual revolutions). The portion of the Moon visible from the Earth depends on the position in its orbit: no portion is visible at the time of the New Moon (*see right*), followed by the Waxing Moon when it is growing in light and more is visible, the first quarter and the Gibbous Moon (¾ moon); when the Moon is full (*central image*), the whole side of the star facing Earth can be seen. The complete cycle of lunar months (the interval between two New Moons) takes 29¹⁄₂ days.

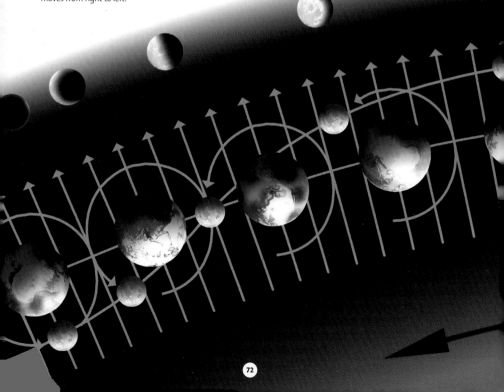

The phases of the Moon

The phase of the Moon in a birth chart is an essential factor in a person's psychological make-up.

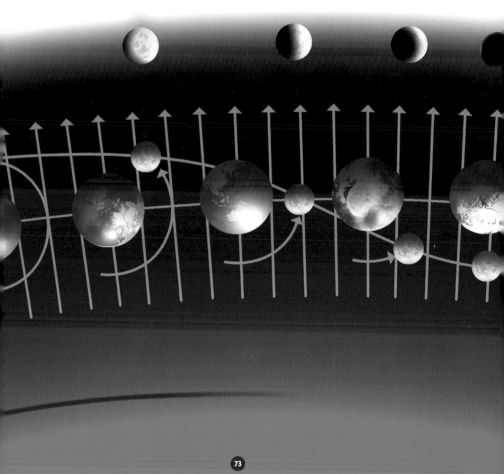 The New Moon corresponds to a period of secrecy, silence, conception and creation.

The Waxing Moon gradually releases energies and develops action.

The Full Moon corresponds to the moment of success (or failure) in projects.

The Waning Moon corresponds to evaluations, lessons learned and the use of past experiences.

Solar and lunar signs

The Sun (the conscious part of the personality) and the Moon (the sensitive part of the being) are two luminaries which describe the human psyche and the way in which the masculine and feminine aspects, yang and yin, combine within the same person.

The moon and versatility

The rapidity of the moon's cycle symbolises variations in mood and daily preoccupations. This is the origin of the term 'lunatic'.

The positions of the planets

Marilyn Monroe

Fundamentally a fragile individual, she was greatly affected by the absence of her father (suggested in her chart by the positions of Saturn and Scorpio in House IV), particularly as her mother was preoccupied above all with herself. Marilyn spent her childhood with foster families, with no solid emotional foundation on which to structure her life (the aspects of the Moon in relation to Saturn and Neptune). Marilyn's father was unknown and in those days that was a disgrace – something that made Marilyn feel guilty throughout her life. It was as though she had been weighed down by a negative judgement since birth, which prevented her from being happy. She managed to counteract this destructive influence to an extent by throwing herself into success and worldly activity, but was not able to escape altogether. 'My heart belongs to Daddy', she sang, with involuntary irony. 'It's great to have a career, but you can't curl up with it at night when you're cold.' She tried to fill this gap with numerous romantic liaisons. Many of her partners were powerful or prestigious, such as the baseball player, Joe Di Maggio, the writer Arthur Miller and, allegedly, President John F. Kennedy. But because she always carried with her an emotional fragility and the chronic sense of need caused by Neptune, she could never be satisfied with any of her romantic relationships and remained a little lost girl until her death at the tragically early age of 36.

Her success, due to her talent as an actress and her ability to seduce the public (particularly men), together with her powerful image as a sex symbol, made Marilyn Monroe into a true legend.

Marilyn Monroe, the vulnerable star (Norma Jean Baker) was an attractive personality suffused with a certain mystery and a subtle charm, determined by the position of Neptune in House I. It was to that same planet that she owed her acting skills, her ability to take on different personalities and, in general, to assume different appearances, sometimes hiding behind them. The conjunction of the moon and Jupiter, linked by a sextile to Venus, reflects the degree to which the actress's charm moved and easily seduced the public, and her image of feminine fragility – both knowing and innocent. Marilyn enjoyed this gratifying relationship with her fans, it undoubtedly made her feel secure and was a substitute for her emotional life which was unfulfilled, as she never had a lasting relationship with a partner who supported and truly understood her.

Interpretation

A more complex interpretation of a birth chart involves the same configurations, which are read several times using a different emphasis in each case. The results are then combined for a fuller picture. For example, here, the Moon (opposed to Saturn) indicates emotional sensitivity and family life, because it is linked to the planets Venus, Jupiter and Mars in Pisces, the Sun (opposed to Pluto) and Mercury. The Moon/Saturn pairing, linked to the ascendant in Libra, suggests health problems and back pains. Positioned in House VI, the Moon relates to professional activity.

Modern astrology (in contrast to deterministic thought) does not attempt to predict the future as though it were independent of our will and we have no control over our destiny, but by revealing psychic aspects and their effects on external reality, it explores potential for personal development and analyses difficulties, identifying possible solutions that can often lead to positive change.

The birth chart

In Mary Smith's birth chart, Aquarius with the ascendant in Libra creates a picture of an idealistic person, who is open to relationships, does not always have her feet on the ground and who wants to fulfil all her dreams at the risk of disappointment. This person is very affectionate, driven by extremely close relationships, and places a great deal of importance on her emotional and maternal life (Venus, Jupiter and Mars in Pisces in House V). She sometimes goes too far and is faced with certain frustrations due, among other things, to daily necessities, which prevent her from living as fully as she would like. This person is not preoccupied by her work, domestic and economic constraints or health matters (Saturn opposed to the Moon). She always reacts spontaneously with the feelings she wants to share with others (the Moon/Aries square of Uranus). In spite of suffering, doubt and difficulties (Saturn in House XII), her capacity for revival is stronger than her apparent fragility (the opposition between the Sun and Pluto). Professionally, this person is suited to activities involving human contact, support and advice (psychological, social, medical fields), as she is highly sensitive and a good listener.

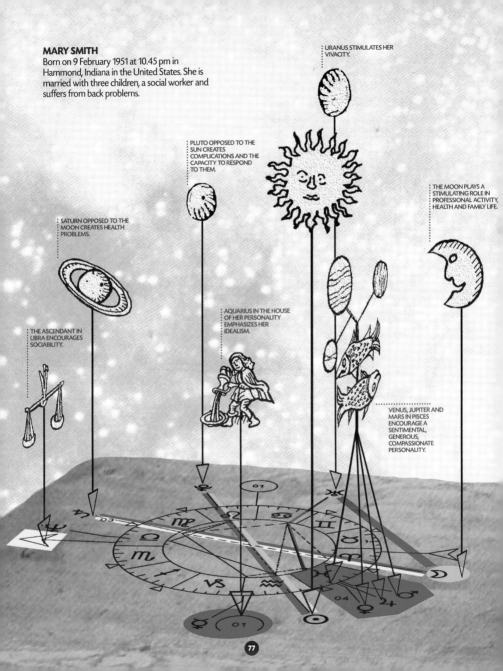

MARY SMITH
Born on 9 February 1951 at 10.45 pm in Hammond, Indiana in the United States. She is married with three children, a social worker and suffers from back problems.

URANUS STIMULATES HER VIVACITY.

PLUTO OPPOSED TO THE SUN CREATES COMPLICATIONS AND THE CAPACITY TO RESPOND TO THEM.

THE MOON PLAYS A STIMULATING ROLE IN PROFESSIONAL ACTIVITY, HEALTH AND FAMILY LIFE.

SATURN OPPOSED TO THE MOON CREATES HEALTH PROBLEMS.

THE ASCENDANT IN LIBRA ENCOURAGES SOCIABILITY.

AQUARIUS IN THE HOUSE OF HER PERSONALITY EMPHASIZES HER IDEALISM.

VENUS, JUPITER AND MARS IN PISCES ENCOURAGE A SENTIMENTAL, GENEROUS, COMPASSIONATE PERSONALITY.

The transits

The transits are one of the most important predictive techniques, as they describe times of key developments and their related influences. They correspond to the movement of the planets through sensitive points in the birth chart, such as the ascendant, the centre of the sky and the personal planets (between the Sun and Mars). The transiting planet triggers the potential of the point with which it comes into contact.

The more personal the transited point (the ascendant, the Sun, the Moon), the slower the transiting planet and the stronger the effect of the transit. For example, Uranus, which revolves around the zodiac in 84 years, takes a lifetime to activate all the points of the birth chart successively. The transit is noteworthy when this slow planet passes over the Moon, causing family changes (such as marriage or divorce). Saturn, with a revolution of 29½ years, can pass through every point in the birth chart three times in a lifetime, and is just as significant despite the reduced impact. Several planets in transit at the same time often interact, linking some points of the chart through certain aspects.

13 May 1981: the attack on Pope John Paul II

Pluto transiting through Mars, the crucially significant ascendant of the birth chart, represents a major transit, as Pluto, which takes 248 years to travel round the zodiac, is the planet associated with important transformations (even death and resurrection). The actual transit took place on 2 May 1981. It suggests violence. Uranus opposed to the Sun is another major transit (on 6 June 1981), which can only occur once in a lifetime. Uranus symbolises sudden, unexpected events, which can be either positive or negative, but in this case it is extremely aggressive, representing catastrophes, threats and possible death (because of the major activator, the Sun). These two transits lie either side of the date of the attack, 13 May. A minor transit (Mars through Venus/Mercury, which takes place every two years), which occurred on 15 May, triggered the effect of the two previous ones.

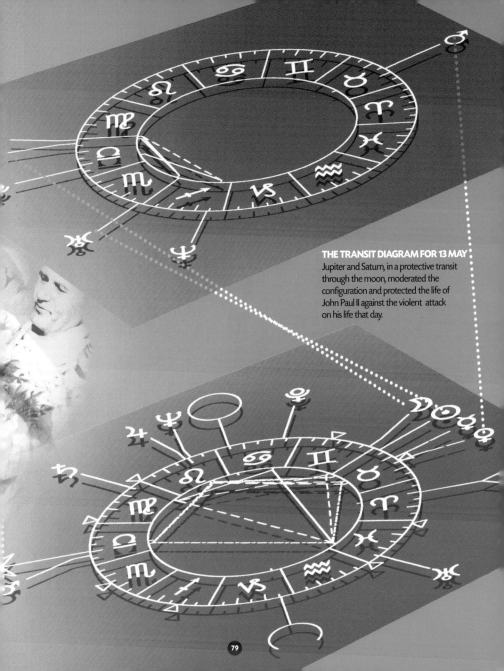

THE TRANSIT DIAGRAM FOR 13 MAY
Jupiter and Saturn, in a protective transit through the moon, moderated the configuration and protected the life of John Paul II against the violent attack on his life that day.

The solar revolutions

The solar revolution, or birthday chart, is the map of the sky at a precise moment of the year, when the Sun returns to its exact initial position in the zodiac. This phase occurs at a different time, however, from the birth phase. And because all the other planets have changed position, the birthday chart is different from the birth chart, with the exception of the Sun's position, which is back in the same sign.

The birth chart can be used to analyse a person's state of mind, his/her potential and the likely course of events over the year to come. This forecast is interpreted both as an independent theme and as a representation of certain capacities within the birth chart. When the two are superimposed, it is possible to identify which Houses and which points in the birth chart are activated by the birthday chart and in what way. For example, the annual ascendant of the solar revolution in House X of the birth chart emphasises the person's professional activity and social success. If the annual ascendant is in birth House XI, it encourages friendship and social activity, and so on. Each annual House therefore draws on the potential of a birth House. The planets within the solar revolution, their positions and their aspects, indicate the action of the individual in practice, taking his birth potential into account.

Isaac Newton and universal gravitation

During the year in which Isaac Newton presented his theory of universal gravitation (1675), his annual ascendant was in Leo, superimposing House X in the birth chart, which symbolises social accomplishment. This position is thought to have favoured the increased recognition of the scientist within his field and confirmed his success amongst the pubic and his contemporaries. Clearly Newton worked extremely hard to obtain this result, combining intuition with his inventive spirit (the Sun in House VI, the House representing work, together with the trine of Uranus in House X, stimulating creativity, the avant-garde and inspiration) with the mathematical rigour and organisation of his thoughts and work (the Moon in Virgo in House III of the intellect). He was quite aware that his work was of fundamental importance (the influence of Saturn) and was able to put his personal doubts aside (square of Saturn) to present the conclusions of his research to the scientists of the time.

THE SOLAR
REVOLUTION

THE BIRTH CHART OF
ISAAC NEWTON
(Source: Matrix)

TIME CHARTS
created on the same day and at the
same time are presented below.

Astrological predictions

Love, a recurrent theme

'Paul asked me to marry him. Should I accept or refuse?' Marie, the lady in question, is symbolised by the Sun (the lord of the current ascendant) and the Moon (the questioner in all cases). Marriage and Paul are represented by House VII and the planets within it (Neptune and Uranus) and the sign of Aquarius. Paul and Marie get on well (the sextile of the Sun with Uranus), but Marie is afraid of being hurt (Moon in Cancer in House XII) because she feels that Paul is non-conformist. Marie is afraid of being deceived (Neptune in house VII) and is divided between two attitudes, one independent (the Sun and Venus in Aries) and the other possessive, because she needs security (the Moon in Cancer; Jupiter, Mars and Saturn in Taurus). Because their relationship is so passionate, there is a danger that it could be stormy (Pluto in House V) and end in separation (Uranus in House VII). However, the things that unite them (complicity, mutual respect) will help them to be open to the world (Mercury and Venus in House IX). The conclusion is therefore a hesitant, 'yes'.

> # Horary astrology responds to specific questions by creating birth charts corresponding to the moment when the questions are asked. For example, if an individual were to ask the question, 'Will I get this new job?', the time at which the question is asked is brought into play when considering the possible outcome. Horary astrology can be applied to all kinds of questions and all types of events. An example of this is given below.

Money and business

'What will be the outcome of my plan to create a partnership with Bill to set up our own company?' Jack, the person asking the question, is symbolised by the lord of the ascendant, the Sun in this case, and its dominant position in the centre of the sky (in Aries) indicates there will be the hoped-for success thanks to his spirit of initiative. He will get on well with Bill (Uranus in House VII), as their two planets are linked in a sextile. Their fruitful cooperation will result in the creation of a sound, active company, which will have everything it needs to prosper in the long term (Jupiter, Mars and Saturn in Taurus in House X). It is necessary, however, to define the legal basis of their partnership clearly, because misunderstandings or adverse effects of their contract could limit their success. Whilst Bill is happy to work in a team (indicated by Aquarius), Jack (Aries) is impatient and sees cooperation as a form of dependence (the square of the Sun with the Moon in Cancer), which he resists. They have to share roles. Jack will become Executive Manager (the Sun/Aries in the centre of the sky), whilst Bill will be in charge of image management, communication and the internal organisation of the company (Uranus, governing advertising and human relations). Frequent, friendly discussions will help them to adapt their professional relations and shared activities will enhance their cooperation (Moon/Mercury trine; Venus/Neptune sextile).

The precession of the equinoxes

There are two zodiacs. The first, the tropical zodiac, is linked to the Earth's revolution (the annual cycle of the Sun), the seasons and human life. The second, the sidereal zodiac, is unchanging (the stars move in relation to each other) and relates to planetary eras.

The tropical, or moving zodiac (measured from the four turning points of the Sun) was used by the original practitioners of astrology, and was of great use in defining climactic conditions. The sidereal zodiac is measured in relation to the fixed stars and moves forward, when related to the calendar, by one day every 72 years. Since it is impossible to pinpoint exactly the limits of the constellations it is difficult to establish exactly when the vernal point changes star sign. However, if we consider the evolution of different peoples throughout the world, it is possible to identify global trends with consistent forms of spirituality. In 4000 BC, the vernal point entered the constellation of Taurus and the period was marked by the prosperity of civilisations (in Egypt, for example) and the worship of the goddess Hathor. Wars and conquests marked the era of Aries in 2000 BC, particularly for the Greeks, and Christianity came to the fore in the era of Pisces.

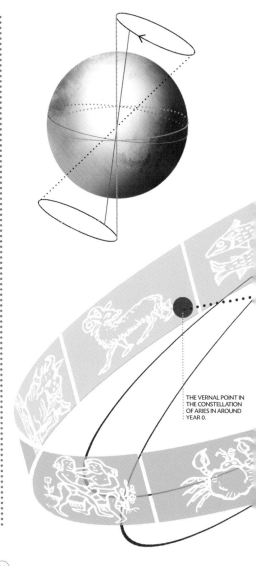

THE VERNAL POINT IN THE CONSTELLATION OF ARIES IN AROUND YEAR 0.

The Earth

The Earth rotates on its axis and is tilted 23° in its orbit. The axis fluctuates in the shape of a cone, like a spinning top which rotates rapidly depending on how fast it is spun, before tilting and rotating on its vertical axis at a slower pace. It takes 25,920 years for the axis to form this cone shape and the Earth's equator, perpendicular to the axis, moves in relation to space and the Earth's orbit at the same time. This means that the line of intersection of these two planes rotates around the centre of the Earth and is projected in space.

THE VERNAL POINT IN THE CONSTELLATION OF PISCES IN AROUND 2000 AD.

The vernal point

The projection of the Earth's equator on the sky passes though the ecliptic (the projection of annual movement in space) at the vernal point, which corresponds to the spring equinox, when the Sun passes through and marks the beginning of the sign of Aries. The tropical zodiac, linked to the Earth's orbit, is defined in this way. It moves at the same time as the axis, but always remains in the same position compared with the revolution of the Earth. The entire system (Earth, axis, equator and zodiac) moves in relation to distant space in the long cycle of 25,920 years. The vernal point is projected on the distant background of the constellations, which forms the sidereal zodiac, by rotating around it whilst moving away. 2,000 years ago, it coincided with the beginning of the Aries constellation. It has since moved by about 25° on the horizon of the stars, moving closer to the constellation of Aquarius, and during the bi-millennium it passed through the constellation of Pisces.

Tarot

According to tradition, the technique of reading tarot was given to mankind by the Egyptian god, Thot. It provides clear, but profound answers using rich symbolism. Like most predictive systems, tarot is based on the idea that all factors must be taken into consideration to build up a complete picture. The cards are drawn at a specific moment and summarise the present situation for the questioner.

The arcanuma ('the plates' or cards in the tarot pack), which are selected in a draw, indicate development. The pack is made up of 22 major and 56 minor arcana. The images and symbols presented by the major ones indicate a stage in the course of a person's life. They begin with the Magician, the beginning of all things, and end with the Fool, the return to chaos and indifference. Each card tells a story which can be deciphered by the reader's intuition but has also been given symbolic meanings which act as a guide for the reader. The minor arcana are divided into four elements like the signs of the zodiac, represented by wands (fire), pentacles (earth), swords (air) and cups (water). They describe the four types of behaviour, will, matter, thought and feelings. The tarot cards are used to answer all kinds of questions, both specific and general.

THE TWELVE-CARD DRAW
This method involves drawing 12 cards and positioning them in the form of an astrological chart, with each card occupying a particular House. This gives a complete image, which can be interpreted like a birth chart. There are other types of draw, which involve the major arcana on their own or combined with 56 minor ones.

THE TWELVE-CARD DRAW

THE CRUCIFORM DRAW

The set of 22 major arcana is cut and distributed face down on the table. Four cards are selected and arranged in the positions indicated (*see left*). After they have been turned over one by one, the values of the four cards are added together. If the total is more than 22, the two figures of the result are added (for example, two + two). The card with the number corresponding to the final result is then removed from the pack and placed in position five.

HOW WILL THE CURRENT SITUATION DEVELOP?

This is what the cruciform draw illustrated here indicates. You are currently depressed, disappointed and feel powerless (the Hanged Man in card one). You are nevertheless able to reflect and identify your resources. You have a feeling that your general situation is changing (the Fool in card two) but, for the moment, the confusion surrounding you is concealing any form of development. You are worried and afraid of making a mistake. Help is in sight (the Magician in card three), a friend will inspire you, you will have an idea or make a decision. The situation is moving in your favour, thanks to your skill and desire to take action. This will produce results which are far better than you had hoped (the Sun in card four), which will bring success in your activities and in your personal and emotional life. A positive period will ensue (the Hierophant in card five), in which you will have a good chance of success and happiness in the plans you make.

1 - THE FIRST CARD represents the person asking the question.
2 - THE SECOND CARD shows the circumstances with which he/she is faced (or the other person if the question concerns a third party).
3 - THE THIRD CARD indicates the way in which external influences affect the situation and how things might be likely to develop.
4 - THE FOURTH CARD provides the answer to the specific question in the person's mind.
5 - THE FIFTH CARD describes the outcome and development of the situation concerned.

Numerology

Since the time of Pythagoras, numbers have been considered rich symbols of universal knowledge. The Hebraic Cabbala links letters with numerical values, forming the basis of scientific calculations which explain the meaning of the universe, mankind and God. In numerology, the letters of the alphabet are associated with Arabic figures, creating an evolving system of divination.

In numerology, the letters of a person's name are converted into figures and added up. This figure is then reduced (by adding together the different figures, for example, three + four) to obtain a single number. The expression number (the total of the letters of the surname and first name) indicates who we are and our behaviour. The active number (the total of the letters of the first name) reveals our personality, while the hereditary number (the total of the letters of the surname) reflects the personality traits that we inherit at birth. The intimate number (the total of the vowels of the first name and the surname) refers to the unconscious and sensitivity. The achievement number (the total of the consonants of the first name and the surname) refers to the external part of the self.

The symbolism of figures

1 Active. The beginning, activity, achievement, affirmation.

2 Receptive. Duality, the search for cooperation and understanding.

3 Creation. Spontaneity, communication, sociability.

4 Achievement. Stability, expression, effort and seriousness.

5 Change. Mobility, freedom, pleasure, independence.

6 Balance. Search for harmony, peace, beauty, family.

7 Internalisation. Isolation, studies, analysis, synthesis, spirituality.

8 Harvest. Justice, growth, knowledge, power, realisation or loss.

9 Accomplishment. Appraisal, ideal, compassion, devotion.

11 The Messenger. Spiritual control, mission, altruism.

12 Greatness. Reason and wisdom (or madness), radiance.

Evaluation grid or star of Venus

The number of repeating letters (which have the same value) is calculated for the first name and the surname. The result, represented in a table (three x three, *see right*), reveals the numbers which are dominant, excessive or lacking. These 'karmic' numbers show where one might need to put in extra effort or be specially aware.

The path of life

This is obtained from the numbers in the date of birth and represents the main lines in a person's destiny.

Forecasts

The personal year is calculated using the birthday date (add together day, month and year), and indicates the tendencies of the year. The personal month is calculated by adding the current month plus the personal year.

Absent zero and sacred numbers

The 0 does not exist in numerology. 11 and 22 are sacred numbers, which represent a character that is so exceptional they are usually reduced to two and four.

EVALUATION GRID

1	1	**2**	2	**3**	1
4	2	**5**	8	**6**	2
7	0	**8**	0	**9**	2

CORRESPONDENCE TABLE

1	2	3	4	5	6	7	8	9
A	B	C	D	E	F	G	H	I
J	K	L	M	N	O	P	Q	R
S	T	U	V	W	X	Y	Z	

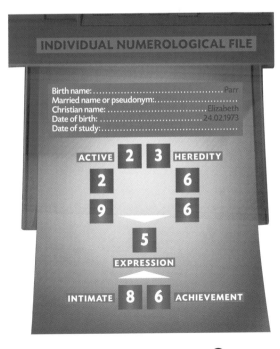

INDIVIDUAL NUMEROLOGICAL FILE

Birth name: .... Parr
Married name or pseudonym: ....
Christian name: .... Elizabeth
Date of birth: 24.02.1973
Date of study: ....

ACTIVE **2** **3** HEREDITY

2 **6**

9 **6**

5

EXPRESSION

INTIMATE **8** **6** ACHIEVEMENT

Example

Elizabeth Parr, born on 24 February 1973, has an expression number of five, which makes her independent and aspire to change. Her active number (11 reduced to two) restricts her passion by enhancing her sensitivity and receptivity, whilst her hereditary number (three) reveals a heritage marked by sociability and creativity. Her intimate number (eight) indicates a strong decision-making capacity and a desire to take action and be dominant, which is expressed diplomatically by her achievement number (six). Her evaluation grid shows the number five in excess (appearing eight times) with a strong need for action, a refusal of constraints and a love of freedom, but she needs to control her impulses. The absent number seven reveals a lack of self-confidence (masked by appearances) and a certain disorder in her ideas and actions. The absence of the number eight indicates difficulties in managing money and a tendency to judge too quickly. Her path of life (number one) favours an active life and enables her to express her dynamism and ambition. However, she needs to make sure that she remains open to others. The personal year for 2000 is number one, which is extremely favourable for starting new projects.

Stones and health

Crystal healing works intuitively and can be practised in a number of different ways – including the permanent placing of appropriate crystals in a room or space (to create a sensation of peace and calm, for example), placing the crystals at key points on the body for the duration of the healing ritual, or simply wearing the crystal as jewellery.

LEO
Golden topaz stimulates a love of life. It helps Leos to radiate light and love. It strengthens the heart, appeases and creates harmony.

VIRGO
Lapis lazuli enhances self-confidence. It increases the Virgo's intuition and favours solidarity. It has a calming effect and alleviates cramps.

LIBRA
The chrysolite generates a feeling of peace. It reassures and balances the sign of Libra and helps to calm anxious or nervous people.

SCORPIO
Haematite gives courage and energy and helps Scorpios to let go and face crises with a positive spirit.

ARIES
Ruby, the love stone, has a purifying effect and allows the sign to strengthen its vitality and become more creative. It also has a stimulating effect, alleviates eye complaints and purifies the blood.

TAURUS
The emerald is the stone of regeneration, peace and love. It creates openness to truth and deep understanding. It alleviates angina and food poisoning.

SAGITTARIUS
The sodalite encourages the consolidation of ideas. It helps Sagittarians to express their ideas more realistically and creates harmony.

CAPRICORN
Tourmaline provides new energy and enhances understanding. It helps Capricorns to achieve their goals and offers protection against falls and negative energy.

GEMINI
Amber welcomes spiritual energy, which appeases and enhances the mental aspect of Gemini. It alleviates respiratory complaints, such as asthma and bronchitis.

CANCER
The moonstone establishes contact with deep emotions and the world of dreams. It favours a person's feminine aspect and fertility.

AQUARIUS
Pale blue fluorite inspires mental aspects. It enables Aquarians to intuitively identify what is right and it alleviates mental suffering.

PISCES
Turquoise promotes wisdom. It helps Pisceans to establish roots, protecting their sensitivity and offering healing forces.

The zodiac figure

Hippocrates, who lived around 400 BC and is considered to be the father of modern medicine, used astrology extensively in order to practise as a physician. In later ages, doctors would consult astrological charts before making a diagnosis. For this purpose, the signs of the zodiac were positioned in descending order from the head to the feet. Each sign has an affinity with the area of the body indicated. This idea forms the basis of medical astrology. The ascendant, which is the point 'through which life enters', shows the potential for health. The corresponding organs are the most sensitive, their correct balance guarantees vitality but these can also be the ones most affected by illness. The presence of the planets in the ascendant sign affect energy. The positions of the Sun and the Moon help determine the form and location of illnesses. Houses VI and XII provide information on the nature of these illnesses and the original genetic make-up of an individual is described by House IV. House VII is associated with accidents and surgical operations. Medical astrology often uses 'alternative' medicine, such as phytotherapy (use of plant medicines), homeopathy (treating 'like with like', or use of drugs which, in a healthy person, would produce symptoms of the disease), acupuncture and the use of crystals and metals.

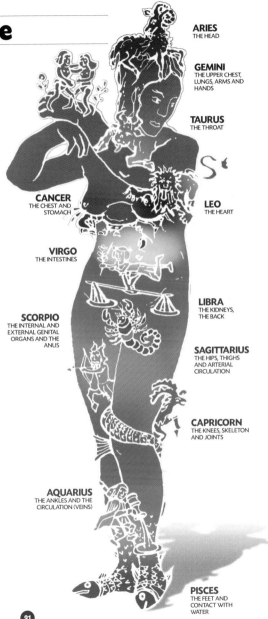

ARIES
THE HEAD

GEMINI
THE UPPER CHEST, LUNGS, ARMS AND HANDS

TAURUS
THE THROAT

CANCER
THE CHEST AND STOMACH

LEO
THE HEART

VIRGO
THE INTESTINES

LIBRA
THE KIDNEYS, THE BACK

SCORPIO
THE INTERNAL AND EXTERNAL GENITAL ORGANS AND THE ANUS

SAGITTARIUS
THE HIPS, THIGHS AND ARTERIAL CIRCULATION

CAPRICORN
THE KNEES, SKELETON AND JOINTS

AQUARIUS
THE ANKLES AND THE CIRCULATION (VEINS)

PISCES
THE FEET AND CONTACT WITH WATER

NYD
TEMPERANCE

IS
ICE

PEORTH
INITIATION

WYNN
JOY

OS
FERTILITY

THORN
STRENGTH

UR
VITALITY

GAR
HARVEST

HAGEL
UNPREDICTABILITY

Runes

The question asked is: 'Will my financial situation improve?' In the past (indicated by the top row of runes), the situation was extremely restricted, Nyd (temperance) indicates a material shortage which led the questioner to reconsider his attachment to his possessions and become more cautious. Is (ice) confirms these restrictions and the solitude that they imply, but Peorth (initiative) indicates that this is simply an illusory appearance and everything can change. The second row (the present) points to extremely positive openings, Wynn (joy) announces a positive change, defined by Os (fertility), such as unexpected money, gifts and advice, which Thorn (strength) will consolidate by protection. Ur (vitality) in the third row (the future) confirms this financial development, which is stabilized by Gar (harvest). However, Hagel (unpredictability) indicates that caution is necessary in order to maintain this situation in the long term.

Runes are presented in the form of small engraved or painted pebbles, which are drawn from a bag one by one.

The word 'rune' comes from the ancient Nordic *run*, which means 'mystery'. The *Edda*, a 12th -century Scandinavian collection of poems which traces the origins of the world, tells of runes being brought to men by Odin. He was so keen to gain knowledge that he agreed to sacrifice his right eye (losing it in the magic Mimir spring, which granted wisdom) and to remain suspended upside down with one foot tied to a sacred yew tree for nine nights. At the beginning of the ninth night, Odin gained insight into the understanding of runes. Runes can give very precise indications when they are drawn, so the reader needs be familiar with the extremely complex and sometimes contradictory, meanings of each one. They do not simply provide a way of understanding life and the path it takes, they also contain magical powers which can be used to influence situations directly (for healing, political advice, etc.).

The example question asked here is: 'I feel tired all the time. Is there anything to worry about?' The three runes drawn are: Lage (water), Ing (accomplishment) and Thorn (strength). The first rune reveals the source of the problem. This tiredness stems from a lack of vitality linked to the emotions, instability and the psychological openness of the questioner. The second rune offers advice on the situation, harmonisation is taking place and needs to be encouraged by rest and internal relaxation. The third rune indicates the development of the problem; strength, as it name suggests, favours the return of more healthy energy, but does not rule out minor problems linked to tensions. The juxtaposition of these three runes provides a response that is generally reassuring, the problem is not serious and the solution is in the hands of the questioner.

Chinese astrology

Chinese astrology is still used a great deal today by the Chinese and Vietnamese to determine the most favourable dates for important events such as marriages, business contracts and any decisions that need to be made. It forms a complete system with Chinese medicine (along with acupuncture, phytotherapy) and Feng Shui (the study of the earth and the habitat).

THE RAT
Charming and creative, succeeds by doing everything to the full.

THE BUFFALO
Practical and silent, a leader who dislikes authority.

THE TIGER
Warm and enthusiastic with a taste for risk, enthusiastic.

THE RABBIT (OR CAT)
Affectionate and faithful, likes peace and comfort.

THE DRAGON
Fiery, powerful and independent, a winner.

THE SNAKE
Charming, wise and reflective, slightly cautious.

THE HORSE
Quick but unstable, aspires to a brilliant life filled with action.

THE GOAT
Dreamy, sentimental and altruistic, needs support.

THE MONKEY
Convincing, curious and crafty, likes to be first.

THE COCKEREL
Proud, organised, authoritative and ambitious.

THE DOG
Sincere, loyal, honest and reliable.

THE PIG
Spontaneous, fun, obstinate and helpful.

In the Chinese calendar, the year ends on the 30th day of the 12th moon with the next one beginning on the following day, the first day of the first spring Moon. This New Year, which is linked to the lunar cycle, occurs on a variable date between the end of January and the middle of February. Each year is associated with one of the twelve signs of the Chinese zodiac from the Rat (1996) through to the Pig (2007), linked to one of the five earthly elements. Every twelve years, the same sign (as shown on the large wheel) is linked to a different element (as shown on the small wheel).

THE FIVE ELEMENTS

The five elements (wood, fire, earth, metal and water) succeed one another (yang and yin) each year: Wood Yang, Wood Yin, Fire Yang, Fire Yin, Earth Yang, Earth Yin, Metal Yang, Metal Yin, Water Yang, Water Yin. These two cycles, of 12 (for the zodiac signs) and five times two, combine to form the sexagesimal zodiac of 60 Chinese years.

FIRE

EARTH

WOOD

METAL

WATER

The Yi Jing

Yi Jing (or I-Ching) means Book of Transformations. It is based on the interplay of yin (feminine, objective, receptive, solitary) and yang (masculine, subjective, outward, social), the elements which determine the creation of human beings when they combine. It contains a series of annotated sentences, 'images' and 'judgements', which describe the present situation, predict future developments and provide advice through poetic formulations, which are universal in terms of their wisdom and philosophy but can also be applied to the specific question.

The traditional draw

Traditionally, 50 *achillea millefolium* sticks (the stems, sorted then cast) are used. A question is asked and the sticks are counted to obtain a figure from which meaning is derived (according to the book). Alternatively, three coins can be used (in which heads are allocated the number two and tails the number three, for example). The coins are thrown six times and the number of heads and tails obtained for each draw corresponds to a yin or yang characteristic (for example, seven determines a yang characteristic and eight a yin characteristic). In each case, the characteristics are listed from bottom to top as the draws are made, and a six-line figure (a hexagram) is created. Sub-divisions, or groups of three, are known as trigrams. The groupings have meanings which indicate the reader's situation. Three of a kind, for example, means that opposite characteristics will be revealed in a new hexagram, which indicates the development or progression of the situation (that is, nine, a complete characteristic, marked by -o-, creates a broken characteristic; six, a broken characteristic marked by -x-, creates a complete characteristic).

Eight trigrams, 64 hexagrams

Eight trigrams summarise the eight possible combinations of three characteristics, some yin and some yang, which can be either complete or broken, depending on the draw. The trigrams are combined in twos to create hexagrams, which produces 64 possible combinations.

Each trigram has a name

Qian: the sky, creator.
Zhen: thunder, the awakener.
Kan: water, the unfathomable.
Gen: the mountain, immobilisation.
Kun: the earth, receptivity.
Xun: wood, softness.
Li: fire, attachment.
Dui: the lake, joyfulness.

Identiying the hexagram drawn

(Refer to the table above for definitions of the hexagram diagrams accompanying the draws.)
Choose the lowest trigram from the vertical list and the highest trigram from the horizontal list, the number of the hexagram sought lies at the intersection of the two lines.

TRIGRAMS Highest / Lowest	Qian	Zhen	Kan	Gen	Kun	Xun	Li	Dui
Qian	1	34	5	26	11	9	14	43
Zhen	25	51	3	27	24	42	21	17
Kan	6	40	29	4	7	59	64	47
Gen	33	62	39	52	15	53	56	31
Kun	12	16	8	23	2	20	35	45
Xun	44	32	48	18	46	57	50	28
Li	13	55	63	22	36	37	30	49
Dui	10	54	60	41	19	61	38	58

First draw: hexagram no. 13

Question:
'Should I follow up on this proposed employment contract?'

 Number 13: 'Community with people'
The judgement:
'Community with people at large. Success.'
The image:
'The sky united with fire: the noble man draws distinctions between things.'
The characteristics (the first one can change):
Nine at the beginning means: the basis of all partnerships must be accessible to everyone involved. Secret arrangements spell misfortune.'
With its flexible characteristic, the first hexagram is transformed into hexagram no. 33 :

Number 33:
'Withdrawal.'
The judgement :
'Success, The noble man keeps his distance from vulgarity, without anger but with careful consideration.'
This confirms that internal honesty must prevail and that dishonest compromises should be avoided.

Second draw: hexagram no. four

Wishing for a fuller explanation, the questioner once again addresses the Yi Jing and draws:

Number four: 'Juvenile folly.'
The judgement:
'Juvenile folly embodies success. It is not I who seek the young fool, but the young fool who seeks me. I inform the first oracle. It is inappropriate for him to ask two or three times. If he is inappropriate, I do not inform him.'
A little annoyed at having been called a young fool, the questioner closes the book. The lesson is clear.

Astrology and psychology

Towards the end of the 1950s, Stanislav Grof, a Czech psychiatrist, obtained some very interesting results with schizophrenic patients. His therapeutic methods involved exploring unknown psychic zones by working with shamans, mystics and using supernatural experiments. In 1965, Grof began to develop a method in the United States which was similar to that of *rebirth* involving hyper-oxygenated breathing, which he called 'holotropic breathing'. He also defined a 'topography' of consciousness, made up of four main elements, or perinatal matrices, which were linked to different phases of the baby's development inside the womb and at birth, as well as to the planets Neptune, Saturn, Pluto and Uranus by symbolic analogy. His research contributed to the development of a form of psychology known as 'transpersonal psychology', which can be linked to the birth chart at the moment of birth. This birth chart can therefore be interpreted in conjunction with a therapeutic approach and personal research. Given that birth, and the months leading up to birth, are recognised as having a permanent effect on a human being's life and personality, this is an important tool for personal transformation.

MATRIX I
Linked to Neptune, The Blessed State.

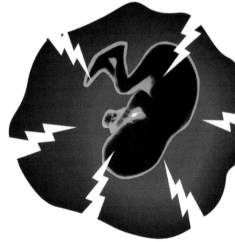

MATRIX II
Linked to Saturn, Painful Effort.

Matrix I

The blessed state of the baby in the uterus. He is safe, weightless, provided with food and oxygen and is in close contact with the mother. This phase relates to situations of plenitude, satisfaction, communion, creativity, imagination, artistic or mystical ecstasy, intoxication of all kinds, and euphoria. On the negative side, it corresponds to situations in which a person loses his bearings, identity, consciousness or vigilance. Neptune describes the aspiration to this integrated state and all the situations that may evoke it.

Matrix II

With the onset of contractions, the uterus suddenly becomes a hostile, hard and turbulent place. An uncomfortable, anxious, restricted environment is created, along with the feeling of being trapped, squashed and suffocated. This phase relates to all hopeless, blocked or threatening situations with insurmountable obstacles, solitude and the passing of time. On the positive side, it corresponds to perseverance, the courage to resist and the triumph of tenacity. Saturn imposes limits and constrains us, but also provides a structure.

Matrix III

Birth and the move through the pelvic/genital barrier. This phase is characterised by the fight for life, suffering, suffocation and extreme danger. It is linked to moments of danger and the imminence of death, a situation of violent crisis, the process of death and resurrection, physical violence, unbridled sexuality and sado-masochistic situations. On the positive side, it is associated with adventure and risk, exceeding personal limits and orgiastic pleasure. Pluto helps us to strengthen our survival instincts.

Matrix IV

When the baby takes its first breath, it is faced with the outside world, light and sound and its mother's arms, in an environment without physical boundaries in which it can move freely. This phase relates to freedom and autonomy, the tensions and efforts that result in victory and success, self-affirmation, joy and sharing. On the negative side, it corresponds to excessive independence, provocative originality and chronic over-excitement. Uranus is the true liberator, paving the way to real life.

MATRIX III
Linked to Pluto, Fighting for Survival.

MATRIX IV
Linked to Uranus, Triumphant Emergence.

Business advice from the skies

Companies can also have their own birth charts, which indicate their strengths and weaknesses, their vocations and their development. The birth chart is created taking into account all the available information and possibilities, on the basis of either the signing of the articles of association or the official establishment of the company. If no specific time can be determined, midday Universal Time (see Glossary, Time Books) on the day that the company is created can be used by default.

The birth chart was calculated for the company that created the Beacons series which includes this book. Since the precise time of the conception of the series was not known, midday was used. The birth chart shows the sun in Capricorn with the ascendant in Aries, a promising combination with great potential. It shows an idea for a collection of books that is designed to be innovative (the ascendant in Aries) with sound content and a desire to explore new horizons (Mercury in House IX, trine with Jupiter and sextile with Mars) and human curiosity. They aim to be eclectic (Mercury in Sagittarius) as well as thorough (Capricorn's influence) and strive to treat each subject authoritatively whilst remaining convivial and accessible (the ascendant in Jupiter, the Moon in Libra).

The combination of these two qualities indicates a favourable reception from the public (same positions, House VII in Libra) aided by strong marketing by the publisher (House XI in Aquarius, with Neptune and Uranus). Certain subjects may give rise to discussion (the ascendant in Aries), and a provocative note is created by Venus (in square with Mars, the Moon opposed to Jupiter). Differences of opinion may prove motivating as they are discussed in detail (the Moon/Libra trine Uranus, Mercury trine Jupiter). Creativity forms an integral part of the collection, which fulfils its goals thanks to its highly innovative design and imagery (northern node in House V).

FIND OUT

THE CONTROVERSY SURROUNDING ASTROLOGY.
THE INFLUENCE OF THE PLANETS ON THE SIGNS OF THE ZODIAC.
ECLIPSES, ASTEROIDS AND THE BLACK MOON.
ARE YOU A BELIEVER OR A SCEPTIC?
ASTROLOGY SOFTWARE.
USEFUL ADDRESSES TO FIND OUT MORE.

Astrology: for or against?

To what extent can astrology be compared with science?

The precession of the equinoxes

The astrophysicist Jean-Claude Pecker, a member of the French Science Academy, believes that astrology is a false science.
'We are frequently brought into contact with horoscopes [...] "Pierre is Taurus" [...] It is claimed that this indicates the character traits of different individuals and even influences their future. But what does it mean when we say, "Pierre is Taurus"? It means that, when Pierre was born, the Sun, which takes a year to revolve around the constellations, was in the part of the sky occupied by the sign Taurus. Pierre's character, according to the horoscope, resembles the mythical imaginary traits associated with the image of the astronomical constellation of Taurus [...] However, the constellation of Taurus was in the sign of Taurus two thousand years ago, but this is no longer the case. Aries has now assumed this position! This simplistic horoscope is therefore a hoax. Given such conditions, horoscopes are meaningless.'

Jean-Claude Pecker, 'Five answers for a keen astrologer', on the Internet site: http://site.afis.free.fr/astrologie.htm

François Biraud and Philippe Zarka, astronomers at the Paris Observatory, do not consider the precession of the equinoxes to be a valid argument against astrology. However, the quoted text concludes that astrology is a false science, making predictions which are unfounded and inaccurate, and its economic and political use is open to criticism.
'The popular argument, according to which astrology is unfounded because it disregards precession (the movement by one and a half signs in relation to the constellations since Antiquity), is very dangerous. Moreover, it is referred to and refuted in most books on astrology. We currently calculate longitudes from 0° to 360°, but this has not always been the case. For a long time they were calculated as 12 signs of 30°. Astrologers have maintained this convention, but it is simply an archaism. The source of the problem lies in the fact that the ecliptic is fixed in space (for the periods of interest to us here), but the Earth's rotation axis has a precession movement of approximately 25,800 years. The equator (terrestrial or celestial) is incorporated in this precession, as are its intersections and the equinoxes with the ecliptic. The precession of the equinoxes therefore stems from the chosen longitudinal source. If we had chosen, in the ecliptic, an origin fixed in space (compared with the stars), the constellations would have remained in their sign over time. However, the influences of the Sun and the Moon on the Earth (through the seasons and the tides) would have gradually become dissociated from the signs and their associated constellations. It was just as logical to measure the positions compared with the intersection of the ecliptic and the equator: the vernal point referred to as "ʏ" in relation to the symbol of Aries. The graduation of the ecliptic in 12 signs of 30° (the tropical or seasonal zodiacs, as distinct from the constellation zodiac) is simply a system of reference in the sky.'

François Biraud and Philippe Zarka,
'Astrology: the theories of two astronomers'.

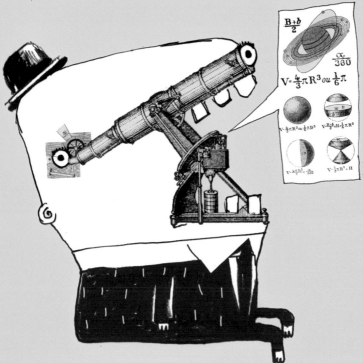

$$\frac{B+b}{2}$$

$$\frac{\alpha}{360}$$

$$V = \frac{4}{3}\pi R^3 \; ou \; \frac{1}{6}\pi.$$

Astrology and science

'It is not always easy to distinguish between astrology and true science. This is not surprising, as at first sight there appear to be many similarities. For example, the horoscope – the objective map of the sky at a given moment – cannot be contested. It is only its astrological interpretation that is dubious. Astrology claims that there is a link between the stars and human behaviour and this does not, a priori, conflict with science. Astrology involves neither supernatural nor metaphysical aspects: in contrast to numerology, divination and fortune-telling (tarot cards, crystal balls, tea leaves).'

François Biraud and Philippe Zarka,
'Astrology: the theories of two astronomers'.

Alain Nègre, Professor of Electronics at Grenoble University, has written about those who try to prove the scientific value of astrology.
'Attempts to prove the validity of astrology do not seek causes or celestial influences, but use statistics to demonstrate the correlation between the astral scheme, symbolized by the map of the skies, and human behaviour. They have been used by rationalist movements, sometimes in cooperation with astrological associations. In all cases, the results invalidate the existence of astral influences on the personality or destiny of human beings. Numerous experiments of this type are recorded in *The Sceptical Inquirer*. [...] Those who try to prove astrology by science perpetuate Bertrand Russell's belief, expounded at the beginning of the century,

was that "the only truth is scientific truth." [...] The truth of astrology cannot be expressed in these terms. For those who examine their birth chart, there is certainly a link between the representation of the universe at the time of their birth and their inner "experience". But, as far as astrology is concerned, this is a symbolic representation of the universe. No symbolic interpretation system is absolutely true. The symbol is characterised by its polysemy and multifarious abundance. It is an opaque language, which can be interpreted numerous different ways. In contrast to the language of science, which tries to explain and present natural phenomena, symbolic language such as that of astrology calls for interpretation and leads us to the very heart of our being. The map of the sky is not a conventional representation, but rather a path in a hidden direction, a sought-after unity, namely unity with the archetypal structure of our being.'

Alain Nègre, *Between Science and Astrology*, S.P.M. publications (1994).

Elizabeth Tessier attempts to elucidate the principle of astrological systems: do the stars influence us or are they a reflection of what is happening on earth?

'Whilst Ptolemy believed in the real influence of the stars, which determines both our body and soul, creating our appearance, morphology, character and everything that forms our destiny, the same could not be said of Plotin, who favoured the idea of stars as signs rather than causes, which tends to imply the idea of the synchronicity and concomitance of celestial and earthly phenomena. "They do not produce things, but only the passive states of the universe [...]", he said, illustrating his point by referring to dancers who move in time with the music of the spheres. Much later, Dante (in his *Divine Comedy*) and Saint Thomas of Aquinas referred to the stars as intermediaries between God and man, whose earthly existence they govern. In reality, although Jung took up and developed the idea of synchronicity in the 20th century, tending to favour the idea of concomitance, the debate remained open. It was between those who believed in the physical influence of the stars and the notion of the stars as signs dissociated from ideas of causality, theories which were not initially mutually exclusive and could coexist [...].

Cause or reflection? Causality or synchronicity? Is it so important after all, once the link has been identified, established and presented? According to Kepler, the father of modern astronomy – an authority on astrology, and also a poet, scientist and pantheistic visionary – who brought together astronomy, astrology and the music of the spheres in a fascinating triptych: "Man's natural soul is no larger than a dot and it is on this dot that the shape and nature of the sky are virtually engraved, even if they are a hundred times bigger".'

Elizabeth Tessier, *Astrologie Passion* , Hachette publications (1992).

Let us conclude with the deep-rooted beliefs of the astrology-lover, Patrice Guinard.

'There are few disciplines which, like astrology, are constantly having to deal with their detractors. This explains why its treatises have often been combined with "defences", particularly since the Renaissance. Astrology has declined in the context of modern culture: its principles are rejected and its methods despised. It has to justify itself in relation to various institutionalized presuppositions, customs, belief and disbelief. There are no university manifestos denouncing psychoanalysis, voodoo, historical materialism or Berkeley's immaterialism. There is no cult, doctrine or practice that has been regularly reviled to such as extent by the pontiffs of the intelligentsia and obliterated by the sceptical deafness of scientists. Could astrology once again be considered as a true alternative to *La pensée unidimensionnelle* (Herbert Marcuse) and *La Société du Spectacle* (Guy Debord)? If so, it is up to the astrologers to become aware of their duty, which consists essentially of conceiving astrology ... rather than trying to sell it in a spirit of dishonestly, cynicism and cowardice generated and maintained by current mentalities.'

Patrick Guinard, 'Le Manifeste.

The influence of the planets

How does the influence of the planets define a particular character? We have already explored how the birth chart can give a clear picture of the influences in play at the moment of someone's birth, and below is a list of the main characteristics associated with the individual planets which are likely to be reflected in the human personality.

The luminaries

The Sun and the Moon, known as 'luminaries', are considered planets in astrological terms.

The Sun

The Sun reveals the characteristics of the sign of the zodiac in which it is positioned.

THE MOON ENTERS THE HOUSE OF VIRGO

The Moon

Aries: vivacity and spontaneity of the emotions, extreme sensitivity, dynamism and enthusiasm.

Taurus: sensuality, focusing on simple, healthy pleasures; attachment and possessiveness.

Gemini: a love of varied relations, diverse interests, ease and rapidity in communication.

Cancer: the typical position of the nursing, protective mother; but also a rich, poetic imagination.

Leo: pride and the image of beauty, a desire for quality and perfection in all areas.

Virgo: discretion and modesty, with a concern to be useful, skilled and helpful.

Libra: a heightened sense of aesthetics, sophistication; typical of artists, lawyers or diplomats.

Scorpio: passion and intensity in emotional and idealistic commitments.

Sagittarius: adventurousness, a willingness to do anything to discover and explore the world.

Capricorn: a tendency towards austerity in order to cultivate sound values.

Aquarius: idealism and open-mindedness to discover new types of relationship.

Pisces: communion, mysticism, dreaminess and hypersensitivity.

These relate to an individual's thoughts, feelings and action.

Mercury

Aries: a keen, intuitive, quick, provocative mentality keen to discover and innovate.

Taurus: the gradual assimilation of knowledge, with sensual, colourful thoughts.

Gemini: a great communicator; a rational, concrete analyst with an eclectic spirit.

Cancer: a poetic spirit, nourished by the memory and emotions; not always objective.

Leo: a belief in truth and the spirit of synthesis.

Virgo: a perfectionist; an analytical spirit with the rigour of a technician who masters his/her subject.

Libra: typically, the lawyer with a love of justice, keen to point out nuances and subtleties.

Scorpio: a committed polemicist, an occultist who strives to unravel mysteries.

Sagittarius: an encyclopedist who creates systems of knowledge and links between different domains.

Capricorn: a person searching for the deep meaning of things using the relevant methods and for a specific field.

Aquarius: an intuitive, inspired mental approach with a concern for universal principles fostering planetary communication.

Pisces: gaining understanding through identification and communication by listening to the music of ideas.

Venus

Aries: seductive, emotionally overwhelming, enthusiastic and passionate.

Taurus: tenderness, loyalty and attachment through lasting love.

Gemini: experimental in their affections, a need for intellectual exchanges in love.

Cancer: love is considered as an emotional fusion; tenderness and mothering.

Leo: a noble, exclusive, idealistic idea of love.

Virgo: modesty, shyness and protected feelings, with compassion and authenticity.

Libra: the charm and pleasure of exchanges form an integral part of feelings.

Scorpio: extreme and passionate.

Sagittarius: a need for large spaces for the overwhelming love that surges up like fire.

Capricorn: feelings develop over time.

Aquarius: a reputation for non-conformism and provocative love, combining friendship with tenderness.

Pisces: love with a capital 'L', which touches on the sublime as it does the ordinary.

Mars

Aries: rapid, fiery decisions; immediate action that can save any situation, provided that it is successful first time.

Taurus: slow to take action or get angry, but unstoppable.

Gemini: disperses anger and shows very little aggression, apart from in words, which can be formidable.

Cancer: a true pacifist by vocation, but moody and expressive.

Leo: the courage and uprightness of a hero.

Virgo: industrious and meticulous, accomplishes considerable tasks with the greatest discretion.

Libra: dislikes confrontation unless fighting for peace.

Scorpio: filled with irrepressible passion, which is impossible to exhaust entirely.

Sagittarius: fieriness and a desire to expend energy in the world without limits.

Capricorn: mastery and perseverance in achieving objectives, whatever happens.

Aquarius: intense creativity and strong convictions underpinning actions, using highly imaginative methods.

Pisces: too kind to display any nastiness, but even the gentlest rebel sometimes.

The social planets

Concerning social behaviour

Jupiter

Aries: confidence and optimism, with dynamic involvement in life.
Taurus: a love of life and willingness to prosper.
Gemini: an eternal teenager.
Cancer: the hospitality of the paterfamilias, kind and debonair.
Leo: a taste for success and honour can lead to excess.
Virgo: an organiser and manager who neglects nothing when finalising projects.
Libra: sociability which can go as far as participating in public life.
Scorpio: a skill for business underpinning determination.
Sagittarius: great explorers and people of note.
Capricorn: ambition channelled into research and crusades.
Aquarius: a belief in humanism or the universal spirit; a dream of unbounded democracy.
Pisces: communion with all forms of creation for a compassionate ideal.

Saturn

Aries: stress and the fighting spirit to achieve goals.
Taurus: stubbornness and a refusal to change opinion.
Gemini: intellectualism, rational thought and objective discourse.
Cancer: focusing on the past, with vulnerable family roots.
Leo: a tendency to stand out through aristocratic pride.
Virgo: meticulous, methodical study to take stock of the world.
Libra: seeking justice to establish a better balance.

Scorpio: authenticity without compromise to transform energies.
Sagittarius: the spirit of a philosopher to open up consciousness.
Capricorn: the wise, political leader, spiritual master and researcher.
Aquarius: having an ideal of perfection; striving towards collective wisdom.
Pisces: sorting and evaluating at the end of a cycle.

The transpersonal planets

Representing the way in which an individual accesses a higher (spirit, technology, etc.) or collective dimension.

Uranus

Aries: the creative impulse and revolution.
Taurus: stabilising in order to create.
Gemini: discovery and communication.
Cancer: the end of traditional emotional structures.
Leo: the urgency of creation.
Virgo: practical, everyday life underpinning revelation.
Libra: when injustice becomes intolerable.
Scorpio: destroying obstacles in order to evolve.
Sagittarius: the strongest dreams are adopted and pursued.
Capricorn: concentration of energy to create change.
Aquarius: the accomplishment of transformations and the wakening of consciousness.
Pisces: in direct contact with the other dimensions of the universe.

Neptune

Aries: inspiration and idealism in action.
Taurus: receptivity to love and artistic sensitivity.
Gemini: attempts to rationalise the irrational.

Cancer: the dream of a lost paradise of emotional union.
Leo: divine love in the heart.
Virgo: attempts to apply ideals practically to daily life.
Libra: the 1960s ideal of peace and harmony.
Scorpio: ability to aspire to other levels of experience.
Sagittarius: the emergence of durable forms of spirituality.
Capricorn: the establishment of the ideal in individual responsibility.
Aquarius: direct contact between intuition and its sources.
Pisces: the return of unity, deserved and striven for.

Pluto

Aries: the way of warriors and militants.
Taurus: the vital instinct at the source of energies.

Gemini: daring to express the unsaid and denounce taboos.
Cancer: fostering sensitivity through internal energy.
Leo: contesting authority in order to establish power more firmly.
Virgo: the transmutation of energies at the centre of the physical body.
Libra: facing the definitive choice between domination or partnership in all relationships.
Scorpio: the liberation of energies trapped at the core of a being.
Sagittarius: the expansion of all human energies.
Capricorn: the strong will that can transform the world.
Aquarius: the true political challenge for a planetary power.
Pisces: a change in the frequency of matter and psychic vibrations.

SATURN IN THE HOUSE OF TAURUS

Lunar nodes, asteroids, segments and the Black Moon

Astrology attributes meanings to other material bodies in the solar system (such as asteroids) and uses certain geometric points in space (such as the Black Moon and the lunar nodes) in its predictions and interpretations.

Lunar nodes and eclipses

All the planets have 'nodes' – meeting points between their orbit and the ecliptic (the earthly orbit) – which are opposed to one another. Western astrology has adopted lunar nodes, which were originally used in Indian astrology, referred to as, 'Ketu' and 'Rahu', or the Head and the Tail of the Dragon. These geometric points generally move in a retrograde direction compared with the Earth (with small direct turns, due to an astrological phenomenon known as 'nutation') in a cycle of 19 years. They are also used in karmic (in which a person's actions in various states of existence are taken into account) astrology, with the southern node symbolising karma and the northern node symbolising dharma. These nodes are of interest in the study of the source of a person's development and indicate the direction to be followed to enable an individual to achieve fulfilment, whilst respecting the person's natural evolution. When a Full Moon or a New Moon occurs in the vicinity of a node, a lunar or solar eclipse occurs. On average, four or five eclipses occur every year (partial, annular or total), but they are only visible from a given point. These eclipses were traditionally interpreted as being evil, as it was feared that the Sun (or the Moon) was being devoured and would never return. In modern astrology, an eclipse is analysed according to the node with which it is associated (north or south), the sign in which it is positioned and even the degree at which it occurs. The general configuration of the sky at that particular moment is also taken into account. The eclipse on 11 August 1999, for example – although it was accompanied by a large planetary square, which could crystallise certain tensions – occurred at the northern node and was therefore highly symbolic for human consciousness in terms of evolution. It indicated an opportunity for collective progress and did not presage catastrophe, in contrast to what the factual astrologers had thought.

Asteroids

The asteroid Chiron (probably the remains of a comet), named after the famous centaur, completes a revolution in around 50 years. Its trajectory, which is off-centre and extended, crosses Saturn's orbit and almost reaches that of Uranus. Chiron is considered to be the link between the distant planets (Uranus, Neptune and Pluto), symbols of transcendence and modernity, and the visible planets which represent human behaviour. In the birth chart, Chiron represents the instructor, the initiator, the teacher and the healer. Another four asteroids can be taken into account, which belong to the 'belt' situated between Mars and Jupiter. The symbolism of these asteroids (Vesta, Pallas, Ceres and Juno) is similar to that of Virgo and Mercury, but is complex so rarely used.

The Black Moon

The Black Moon corresponds to the second seat of the Moon's orbit (the ellipse) and coincides, from a geocentric point of view, with the Moon's zenith. It completes a revolution in nine years. Since the first seat of the Moon's orbit is the Earth, the Black Moon symbolically represents the invisible counterpart of our planet. In the birth chart it symbolises things that are left unsaid, experiences that have not been accepted and emotions that have been pushed into the unconscious before being experienced. It therefore evokes the victory of negation and denial over consciousness. Its position (with the planets linked to it by aspects) reveals functions or capacities, which

sometimes disappear suddenly (personality flaws). The Black Moon, representing the hidden side of an individual, symbolises the shadow and is often associated with traumatic sexual experiences. It is a highly karmic point and gives indications, with the southern node, of unsettled situations. In a different approach, it represents the 'ghosts' handed down through generations of a family until one of the descendants eliminates them.

111

Current trends

It is said that there are as many ways of practising astrology as there are astrologers and this is not far from the truth. It is nevertheless possible to identify general trends, in addition to national trends, some of which intermingle, whilst others vary according to the subjects studied and the interpretation methods and techniques used.

Factual astrology

Factual astrology attempts to predict future events. It is generally deterministic and implicitly considers man to be powerless in the face of destiny, which is seen as being independent from him. It has been made popular by the media and attracts criticism from the fiercest opponents of astrology as such specific predictions relating to world or public events attract a great deal of scorn if they miss the mark.

Psychoanalytical astrology

This method applies astrology to the vision of psychoanalysts, particularly Freudians. According to this system, the different Freudian stages, complexes and tendencies in a person's life can be associated with planets and signs.

Characterological astrology

This is similar to psychoanalytical astrology and consists of analysing the character and behaviour of people on the basis of the birth chart. It is sometimes used for recruitment.

Medical astrology

Used by naturopaths, hypnotists and healers, this approach could be used in addition to conventional medicine, particularly for prevention and treatment selection, but is opposed by the medical profession. It involves consulting a chart in which signs of the zodiac are related to specific parts of the body.

Scientific astrology

Scientific astrology attempts to prove and verify the basis of astrology using statistics and is strongly opposed by scientists. Current research concerns studies related to twins.

Humanist astrology

Humanist astrology is of American origin and was developed by Dane Rudhyar. It focuses on the position of the human being in a precise social context. Alexander Ruperti was a brilliant proponent of this theory in Europe.

Cosmobiological astrology

Developed by Reinhold Ebertin based on the energising vision of man, it focuses on the importance of genetic, sociological and environmental factors on human development.

Spiritualist astrology

This integrates man's spiritual dimension according to different Eastern and Western schools. It is referred to in a large number of fields. The theosophist Alice Bailey has written numerous works on this subject.

Karmic astrology

Often linked to spiritualist astrology, this form of astrology explores the influence of karma (experiences in previous existences) on present life. It is rich in terms of explaining the causes of a situation but rather limited in its ability to predict future events due to its tendency to focus on the past. Genealogical astrology, which is similar in nature, studies the effects of trans-generational family experiences on an individual.

Inspirational astrology

This combines astrology, spirituality and/or *channelling*. Intuition mingles with a technical approach to create the birth chart.

World astrology

A traditional approach which focuses on the evolution of the world rather than individuals – major events such as wars, catastrophes, revolutions and peace treaties. British authors, Charles Harvey and Nicholas Campion have written on this subject.

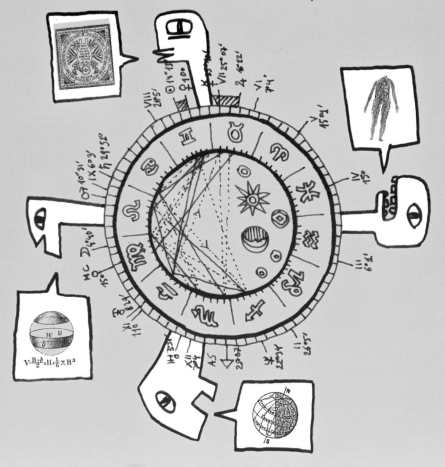

Sceptic or enthusiast?

Find out how much you know by answering the following questions. To find out which way you lean, read the responses below.

Do you know your ascendant sign?

● I am Taurus/Leo (or Virgo/Aries, etc).

■ What's that?

▲ My astrologer has corrected the time of my birth. He thinks that I need to add on ten minutes and that the ascendant is 24°30' from Pisces.

Did you ask your partner what their star sign was before accepting or arranging a meeting?

● Yes, I get on better with fire and air signs.

▲ I met my partner through an advert that asked about preferred dates and times of birth.

■ No, I asked for their telephone number.

Do you have your astrological forecast drawn up every year?

■ I don't believe that it's possible to predict things. I manage my life quite well on my own.

▲ Yes, every year. I take stock every month using my transits.

● I read the forecasts in *Cosmopolitan*, *Vogue*, *Prediction* and *Destiny* magazines.

Do you read your horoscope every day?

▲ No. It isn't detailed enough and only takes the solar sign into account.

● Very often.

■ Are you serious?

Do you believe in the influence of the stars?

● Yes, it seems to work.

■ We are conditioned by heredity, education, the environment and our experiences. I think that's quite enough!

▲ It isn't an influence, but things happen as though it was.

If an astrologer told you that you were going to have an accident if you went out, what would you do?

■ The suggestion alone could induce an accident. It's important not to be too credulous.

● You never know. I would stay at home or be very careful crossing the road.

▲ It isn't as simple as that. I would ask them which transits they had based their forecast on.

Under what circumstances would you consult an astrologer?

● The last time it was because I suspected that my partner had met someone else.

▲ To clarify difficult situations, such as if I was planning to change jobs.

■ I would have to be convinced of the validity of their analyses first.

If you were expecting a baby, would you take an interest in its birth chart?

● A lady comes to the rooms in the maternity hospital and draws up birth charts. It's very handy.

■ Definitely not at such an early stage. It might make us treat the baby in the wrong way.

▲ We will have a stop-watch to note the time of the baby's first cry to the nearest second.

If you were told that your birth chart indicated a problem in a particular area, how would you react?

▲ I would think it was quite possible. And you could find a solution by analysing the configuration.

■ How could things be predefined?

● Don't talk about bad luck! It depresses me.

What do you think about Paco Rabanne's prediction that the Mir space station was going to fall on Paris during the eclipse in August 1999?

● Paco Rabanne remembers his previous lives. I would like to know about mine.

▲ He was misinformed. That type of announcement is extremely harmful for serious practitioners.

■ Just that it has once again been proven that this type of forecast is nonsense.

IF YOU HAVE MAINLY:

■ *You are rational and sceptical and do not believe in astrology. But perhaps you have only seen its bad side so far?*

● *For you, astrology is like pleasant background music. Take care not to be taken in by superstition and maintain your discernment.*

▲ *You are a true devotee! You are well-informed, but take care not to let it rule your life. Make sure that there are still some surprises in store for you and try to relax.*

Astrology software

In order to acquire all the functions that are essential for a professional result, you should consider investing in top-of-the range products. But if you just want an introduction to astrology, you can content yourself with free software, which can be downloaded from Internet sites or ordered by post.

Go forth and predict

2

1
Insert disk

ASTROLOGY SOFTWARE			
NAME	SYSTEM	PRICE	COMMENTS
Astrolabe	Dos	Free	Precise, complete and easy to use. Excellent. Downloadable.
Astrolog	Dos, Windows, Mac, Unix	Free	Probably the best free software on the market. Downloadable.
Junior Jyotish	Windows 95/98 NT4.0	Free	An introduction to Indian astrology. Downloadable.
Astroscan	Windows	Free	Full range of features. Quite powerful.
AstrolDeluxe	Windows	$119	
AstrolDeluxe ReportWriter	Windows	$149	Simple and intuitive.
King of Stars	Windows 95	Sold by module. Special offers. Complete $140	
Kairon	Mac	Free	Includes tropical and sidereal zodiacs.
Win*star 2.0 Win*star Express	Windows 95/98/NT	£189 £79	The most comprehensive astrology programme running under Windows. For professional and amateur.
Goravani Jyotish	Windows Mac	Around $295	Indian astrology. Excellent. Downloadable demonstration available.
vAstro	Windows	2 parts £29.99 each	For the semi-professional, intermediate or beginner.
Solar Fire	Windows	$295	Traditional or classical astrology. Downloadable from the Astrolabe site.
Time Cycles Research	Mac	$150–$300	Professional or very serious.
Astro 22 Astrology		Free	Beginner to advanced. Downloadable.
Astrology for Windows	Windows	$26.50	Easy-to-use, accurate.
Astro-World	Windows	$40, registration $100, professional version	Mainly for the casual horoscope reader.
TimePassages	Windows, Mac	$100–200	Easy-to-use, fully interactive.

Learning about astrology

Many astrology enthusiasts have learnt by themselves from books. However, group or one-to-one courses can speed up the learning process and answer many of the questions that are often raised. Internet sites offer courses or publications and links to other sites. The services listed below also provide consultations and arrange personal interviews.

Training courses

FACULTY OF ASTROLOGICAL STUDIES
54 High Street
Orpington
Kent
BR6 OJQ

Correspondence courses:
Certificate: £295
Intermediate ; £230
Diploma: four blocks of
£290 each
Evening classes: £340 for 24
Tel. 07000 790 143

NOEL TYL MASTER'S DEGREE CERTIFICATION COURSE IN ASTROLOGY

Correspondence course for students with experience and good astrology software.
19 in-depth lessons: $650
www.noeltyl.com
Tel. 001 480 816 0000

THE ASTROLOGICAL PSYCHOLOGY INSTITUTE
Correspondence course
Two-year diploma course
Workshops
Varying Prices
www.api-uk.org
Tel. 01565 651 131

MAYO SCHOOL OF ASTROLOGY
Jackie Hudson
Alvana Gardens
Tregavethan
Truro
Cornwall
TR4 9EN

Correspondence course only
Certificate: £180
Advanced preparatory: £150
Advanced diploma: £350
Tel. 01872 560 048

INSTITUTE OF PROFESSIONAL ASTROLOGY
Skysage Publications
PO Box 367
Kentfield
Ca 94914
USA
Correspondence course
Five levels with continuous online support
www.skysage.com
Beginner
Intermediate
Advanced
Professional
Master
$249 for 12 lessons, first lesson free

THE ASTROLOGY COMPANY
Master of Astrology –
comprehensive correspondence course leading to professional practice
Beginner
Intermediate
Advanced
Professional
8 lessons: £250
16 lessons: $500
24 lessons: $675
www.theastrologycompany.com

AMERICAN INSTITUTE OF VEDIC STUDIES
P.O. Box 8357
Santa Fe
NM 87504-8357
USA

Beginners in-depth correspondence course
Approximately 40 lessons
Course, plus material: $350
www.hinduism.about.com/cs/astrology/

Internet

ABOUT ASTROLOGY
With links to related sites and covering a wide range of subject areas including Western, Chinese and Vedic astrology. Includes chat section and recent articles, plus guidance on how to calculate birth charts.
astrology.about.com/science/astrology/mbody.htm

THE ASTROLOGICAL ASSOCIATION (UK)
The official site for the association. Contains a directory of astrologers throughout the world, plus information, extracts from the association's journal, details of books.
www.astrologer.com

THE AMERICAN FEDERATION OF ASTROLOGERS
The official site for the federation: contains links, details of books, lots of information.
www.astrologers.com

ASTROLOGY ON THE NET
1,500 links to astrological sites. A mine of information.
www.whatsonthe.net/astromks.htm

ASTROLOGY WORLD
Resources, articles, databases, information and contacts.
www.astrology-world.com

COSMIC PATTERNS
Astrology software and services, including news and upgrades, online chart-ordering service, Avalon College details.
www.astrosoftware.com

THE CENTRE FOR PSYCHOLOGICAL ASTROLOGY
Provides workshops and professional training programme linking humanist and transpersonal psychology.
www.astrologer.com/cpa/

EQUINOX
The site for the Astrology Shop (based London, UK), offering personalised birthcharts, psychological horoscopes, the astrological library. Also includes Australian Astrology website.
www.astrology.co.uk/index.htm

ONLINE COLLEGE OF ASTROLOGY
Leading site for education for professional astrologers, including book search service and details on events, lectures and special classes.
www.astrocollege.com

THE MOUNTAIN ASTROLOGER
The site associated with the magazine. Articles, hypertext links. Very interesting.
www.mountainastrologer.com

SPIRITWEB
Includes definitions and history of Vedic and Western astrology, chart calculation, sections on past lives and reincarnation, chanelling, etc.
www.spiritweb.org/spirit/astrology.html/

WEB SITES ASTROLOGY
Links to sites on astronomy, astrology, calculation, publications, etc. Extremely rich.
pages.prodigy.net/astrology/astrolog-htm

YOUR PLANETS
Personalised Vedic astrology, including chart-orderinf service.
www.yourplanets.com

THE ZODIACAL ZEPHYR
Articles, links, database, bibliography, information on calculating birth charts, etc.
www.zodiacal.com

Further reading

Western astrology, general

The Astrology File, Gunther Sachs. Orion (1998). Containing wide research and statistics demonstrating the link betweeen star signs and human behaviour.

Astrology, a Key to Personality, Jeff Mayo. The C.W. Daniels Company, UK.

Astrology for Living, Sasha Fenton. Collins & Brown (1999).

Astrology, The Next Step, Maretha Pottenger. ACS Publications. (8th Edition, 1999.) Complete horoscope interpretation.

Astrology Revealed, Paul Fenton-Smith. Simon & Schuster, Australia.

Brady's Book of Fixed Stars, Bernadette Brady. Samuel Weiser, Inc., (1998). Complete book on the fixed stars, combining modern chart interpretation with ancient Egyptian and Greek methodology.

Do-It-Yourself Astrology, Lyn Birkbeck. Element (1996).

Jonathan Cainer's Guide to the Zodiac. Piatkus (1997).

The New Astrology, The Art and Science of the Stars, Nicholas Campion and Steve Eddy. Bloomsbury (1999).

How to Read Your Star Signs, Sasha Fenton. Thorsons (1998). Integrating readings for Sun, Moon and Rising signs.

Mix and Match, Sun and Moon Signs, Richard Craze. Godsfield Press, UK.

The Modern Textbook of Astrology, Revised Edition, Margaret E. Hone. L. N. Fowlers & Co Ltd.

The Origin of the Zodiac, Rupert Gleadow. Jonathan Cape (1968).

True as the Stars Above, Neil Spencer. Gollancz (1988).

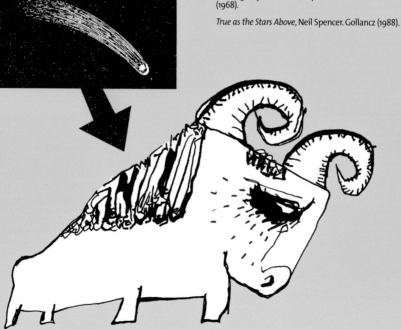

Astrology and analysis

Astrology, Psychology and the Four Elements, Stephen Arroyo. CRCS Publications (1975). Astrology as used in counselling.

Astroanalysis, The American Astroanalysts' Institute. Berkley Books, USA. Practical handbooks with individual titles covering each of the zodiac signs.

Other approaches

Eastern Systems for Western Astrologers. Samuel Weiser, Inc. (1997) Collected essays on subjects ranging from the I-Ching to Vedic Astrology by a range of acknowledged experts.

Chinese Astrology, Man-Ho-Kwok. Tuttle, Boston. (1997).

Simple Chinese Astrology, Damian Sharp. Conari Press, USA.

Journals

The Astrological Journal, published by The Astrological Association (see below).

Old Moore's Almanack

Old Moore's Almanack claims to have brought out an issue every year since 1697. Its contents range from vague predictions of world events to factual tables of high tides and lighting-up times. It has an out-of-doors flavour, with special guides for anglers and advice on when to sow and reap in the garden. Celebrity features fill the rest of the pages.

Astronomy magazines

Astronomy Now, PO Box 175, Tonbridge, Kent TN10 4ZT, England.

Sky and Telescope, PO Box 9111, Belmont, MA 02178-9111, USA.

Useful Addresses

The Astrological Association, 396 Caledonian Road, London N1 1DN, UK.

American Federation of Astrologers, PO Box 22040, Tempe, AZ 85285-2040, USA.

Federation of Australian Astrologers, 20 Harley Road, Avalon, NSW 2107, Australia.

Quotations

The stars rule men but God rules the stars.
> Cellarius, *Harmonica Macrocosmica: Preface* (1661)

... we make guilty of our disasters the sun, the moon, and the stars: as if we were villains by necessity; fools by heavenly compulsion; knaves, thieves, and treachers, by spherical predominance; drunkards, liars, and adulterers by an enforced obedience of planetary influence...
> Shakespeare, *King Lear*

There's some ill planet reigns:
I must be patient till the heavens look
With an aspect more favourable.
> Shakespeare, *Winter's Tale*

A man gazing at the stars is proverbially at the mercy of the puddles on the road.
> Alexander Smith, Dreamthorp: *Men of Letters*

(All the above taken from Stevenson, *The Home Book of Quotations*)

In cases of difficult psychological diagnosis I usually get a horoscope...I very often find that the astrological data elucidated certain points which I otherwise would have been unable to understand.
> Carl Jung, 1948

The fault, dear Brutus, lies not in our stars but in ourselves that we are underlings.
> Shakespeare, *Julius Caesar*

Experience tells us that the nearest constellations have a decisive influence on weather, vegetation and so on; we can only progress outwards step by step and it is impossible to say where the effect ends. Indeed, astronomers find everywhere disturbance of one constellation by another.
> Goethe, 1798

Practically every major move or important decision was agreed with a woman in San Francisco who cast horoscopes. Shortly before the President was shot in an assassination attempt in 1981, this astrologer prophesied that 'something bad' would happen to Ronald Reagan.
> Donald T. Regan, *For the Record*

Millionaires don't believe in astrologers, billionaires keep them on the payroll.
> J.P. Morgan

ASCENDANT

The sign that is present at the moment of birth. It corresponds to the way in which the individual expresses himself and his personality. It coincides in the birth chart with the horizon in the East.

ASPECT

A specific angle linking two planets or two points in the birth chart (compared with the Earth, at the centre of the circle). The aspect combines the effects of the two planets in a particular way.

BIRTH CHART

Another name for the map of the sky. Astrologers work with birth charts, which are created for a specific place on a given date and at a particular time.

THE CENTRE OF THE SKY

Or midheaven, or the highest point the Sun reached at midday on the day of birth. It marks the start of House X, corresponding to the socio-professional situation.

CONFIGURATION

All the elements (planets,
signs, aspects) in the birth chart, which interact with each other.*

CONJUNCTION

The aspect of 0°, when two planets are located in the same place. This aspect combines the effects of the two planets. The result obtained depends on their respective natures.

CONSTELLATION

A fixed group of stars. Each group has a name. The stars in the grouping are not necessarily positioned close to one another, but appear to be due to the perspective from Earth.

THE DEPTHS OF THE SKY

In the birth chart, this corresponds to the nadir (the Sun's position at midnight). It symbolises a person's roots or origins.

DESCENDANT

The opposite to the ascendant. The horizon in the West at the time of birth. It concerns relationships with other people.

ECLIPSE

Occurs when the Earth, the Moon and the Sun are perfectly aligned. Solar eclipses occur at the time of the New Moon (the Moon hides the Sun) and lunar eclipses occur
when the Moon is full (the Earth's shadow conceals the Moon).*

ECLIPTIC

The plane of the Earth's orbit where eclipses occur and which serves as a reference point.

ELEMENTS

Fire, earth, air and water. Each one coincides with a psychological or cosmic dimension: fire with action and will; earth with matter and instinct; air with exchanges and thought; and water with sensitivity and emotionalism. Each sign is associated successively with one of these elements (Aries, fire; Taurus, earth, etc).

THE EMERALD TABLE

Teachings (by an unknown author) from which all the occult sciences originate, including astrology.

EPHEMERIS

The ephemeris is a book which records the sidereal times (measured by the fixed stars) and the position of each planet in the solar system every day in terms of longitude. Indications of the date of birth are essential for the creation of a birth chart, whilst for forecasts, the future years are important. It is therefore necessary to use an ephemeris, which covers a period of at least a century. They are presented as tables of figures recorded month by month, year after year.

EQUINOX

The moment when night is equivalent to day in the spring and in the autumn. In the West (though not in India) the zodiac begins from the vernal equinox, (the spring equinox of the northern hemisphere) when the sun passes through Aries as 0°.

FINANCIAL ASTROLOGY

The use of the birth chart to determine the best investments and an individual's financial management.

GEOCENTRIC

With the Earth at the centre. Our astrology is geocentric. We look at the sky from our earthly base, in other words from the perspective of the Earth.

HEAVENLY BODY

Name used in astrology to denote the bodies (material and immaterial) in space, including stars, planets and satellites.

HELIOCENTRIC

With the Sun at the centre. Looking at the sky from the perspective of the Sun. It is possible to create heliocentric birth charts for research purposes.

HOROSCOPE

A word that comes from the Greek horoscopos, meaning, 'that considers the time' of birth to calculate the birth chart. (see birth chart).

HOUSE

The 12 Houses are defined by a diagram superimposed onto the birth chart and read in a clockwise direction from the ascendant. Each House corresponds to a particular area of activity.

THE HOUSE TABLE

Indicates the position of the Houses in terms of zodiacal longitude starting from the centre of the sky (the zenith) according to the latitude of the place of birth. These positions are determined according to a sidereal (measured according to the fixed stars) time, which is calculated using the time of birth, the longitude of the place of birth and the sidereal time of the day

obtained from the ephemeris. These positions indicate the position of the ascendant.

INTERCEPTION

An intercepted sign is one which appears totally inside a House and not on the cusp. It indicates areas in which an individual will need to be self-supporting and not reliant on others.

LORDSHIP

The association between a planet and one or two signs of the zodiac. The planet is said to be the 'lord' of the sign. This creates different hierarchical levels of energies in the birth chart and logical links between the sectors.

LUNAR NODES

Geometric points opposed to one another, which stem from the intersection of the planes of the lunar and territorial orbits (the ecliptic). In astrology, they represent the tensions and energies in a person's life and can indicate a potential path of spiritual development. The South Node represents a person's past or heredity and the North Node represents a person's possibilities for growth and their future.

THE MAP OF THE SKY

Another name for the birth chart. It is a true representation of the solar system at the time of birth.

NATAL ASTROLOGY

The creation of the birth chart to in order to study the positions of the planets at the time and place of a person's birth.

OPPOSITION

The aspect (angle) of 180°. Two planets facing each other will, depending on their nature, conflict with, complement or counterbalance each other.

ORBIT

The trajectory of a planet around the Sun in the form of an ellipse. It is in more or less the same plane for all planets, that of the ecliptic.

PLANETS

Nine material bodies in the solar system. In the birth chart, the luminaries (the Sun and the Moon) are included. Since the birth chart is centred on the Earth and the latter does not count, ten planets are taken into account.

THE PRECESSION OF THE EQUINOXES

Retrograde movement of the vernal point in space, which completes a revolution in approximately 25,800 years.

PROGRESSIONS

Indicate an individual's development through life and are linked to Transits (which act as triggers for this). A progressed chart, different from the birth chart, reveals this.

QUALITIES

These relate to the point in a season where the sign falls (see Modes). Cardinal signs (at the beginning of the season and tending to be self-motivated and ambitious, generating activity) are Aries, Cancer, Libra and Capricorn. Fixed signs (mid-season, and tending to be determined, stable) are Taurus, Leo, Scorpio and Aquarius. Mutable signs (end of the season, tending to be

versatile and resourceful) are Gemini, Virgo, Sagittarius and Pisces.

RECTIFICATION

A method in which an astrologer can find out an individual's birth time (if not known), based on events in their life.

RETROGRADE

The opposite of direct. It refers to an (external) planet which appears to be moving away from Earth. In reality, the Earth is moving faster and is overtaking it. For Mercury and Venus (internal planets), this movement occurs when they are on the same side of the Sun compared as the Earth.

REVOLUTION

The time that it takes a planet to travel through the zodiac or rotate around the Sun.

RISING SIGN

The sign which is rising in the East at the time of birth. It corresponds with the Ascendant, and represents how the individual presents themselves to the world, influencing such things as self-expression, appearance, outwardly perceived identity.

SECTORS

Another name for Houses.

SEXTILE

Aspect (angle) of 60° which corresponds to the harmonisation of the planetary functions. In terms of an individual's life, this angle can represent an opportunity for development.

SIGN

The portion of 30° of the zodiacal band (which is made up of 12 signs). Each sign has numerous particularities and tendencies (as defined in Chapter five). The solar sign is the one in which the Sun is located at the time of birth. All 12 signs are, however, present and active in every birth chart. They represent animals, objects or people and symbolise tendencies linked to every part of the year.

SOLSTICE

The time and point when the sun is farthest from the equator. The Winter Solstice (normally 21 or 22 December) corresponds to the entry of the sun in Capricorn and the Summer Solstice (21 June) corresponds to its entry in Cancer.

SQUARE

The 90° aspect revealing tension or conflict, which can create restrictions or blocks, but which can also energise the birth chart.

STARS

Term used in astrology to denote distant celestial bodies other than the Sun. They are 'fixed' because their apparent movement is extremely slow compared with that of the planets in the solar system. Stars are grouped together in constellations, which bear the same names as certain signs of the zodiac.

SYNCHRONICITY

The idea that all things in the universe are interconnected, as expressed in the work of the psychoanalyst, Carl Gustave Jung, who believed that we share the energies present in the wider universe at the time of our birth.

TIME BOOKS

Time books give universal times for all the countries in the world according to official times (which depend on the time zone of each country.) The exact UT (universal time) must be known in order to calculate the Houses in a birth chart.

TRANSIT

The movement of a planet over a particular point in the birth chart, triggering events, key decisions, etc.

TRINE

A major aspect of 120° which indicates strong interaction between the planets and is considered favourable as their signs usually share the same elements. They can represent strengths which a person may be generally unaware of because they seem to come so easily.

THE VERNAL POINT

The point in the ecliptic that corresponds to the origin of the zodiac, or 0° from Aries. It coincides with the spring equinox when the Sun is located in that specific point. potential with respect to their career.

YI JING (I-CHING)

Or the Book of Transformations. A book of Chinese wisdom which contains advice on dealing with human, social and political situations.

YIN AND YANG

Considered in the East as, respectively, female (receptive, inward, solitary) and male (creative, outgoing, social) principles, which are at the root of the existence of the world and all beings. Yin and Yang represent the balance of characteristics in an individual's personality.

ZODIAC

All the planets are located in roughlt the same circle, which can be identified by the twelve signs of the zodiac. Counting from 0° to 360°, each sign occupies 30°.

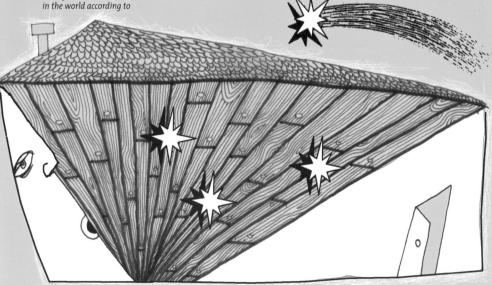

Contents

Fact ⟫ 2–12
Fun facts and quick quotes

Discover ⟫ 13–48

Look ⟫ 49–62
The signs of the zodiac from Aries to Pisces

In practice ⟫ 63–100

Find out ⟫ 101–125

Credits

P.14, Stêle de Kuduru/AKG Paris; **P.16**, *Atlas, Astrologie, la Géometrie et le dieu Nil*, painting by Giambattista/AKG Paris; **P.19**, *The royal family of Aménophis IV Akhanaton offering a sacrifice to Aton, the Sun god*/Magnum; **P.20**, *Ptolemy*, Greek astronomer, oil on wood, by Juste de Gand and Berruguete Pedro, photograph Arnaudet/RMN; **P.23**, *Le serpent infini*, Indian miniature, photograph, Jean-Louis Nou/AKG Paris; **P.25**, *Le Grand Faîte et les 8 trigrammes*, photograph, Roland and Sabrina Michaud/Rapho; **P.26**, *Codex Borbonicus*, photograph R. Percheron/Artephot; **P.29**, Arabic manuscript, Bibliothèque Nationale, France; **P.31**, *L'Astrologue*, painting by Gérard Dou/AKG Paris; **P.34**, *Atlas Petrified*, gouache by Sir Edward Burne-Jones/The Bridgeman Art Library; **P.34**, *Le Nouveau Monde*, painting by K. Juan/Giraudon; **P.36**, *Sister Gabriel*, photograph Smith Gavin, FSP/Gamma; **P.40**, Pandit Anand Shankar Vyas, famous astrologer, photograph Roland and Sabrina Michaud/Rapho; **P.43**, *Supper at Emmaus*, by Caravaggio, digital composition by Gandee Vasan/Fotogram-Stone Images; **P.44**, Pic du Midi Observatory at night, photograph Olivier Sauzereau/Explorero; **P.47**, *Aquarius*, painting by Sabira Manek/The Bridgeman Art Library; **P.48**, Detail of an English window representing the creation of the universe/The Bridgeman Art Library; **P.50 to 62**, miniatures of a 13th-century manuscript from southern Italy, photograph Jean-Loup Charmet; **P.70**, photograph Keystone and D.R.; **P.71**, photograph Photothèque Hachette; **P.74**, detail Elliott Erwitt/Magnum; **P.80**, portrait Newton/Photothèque Hachette; **P.64 to 85, 90 to 95, 98 to 100**, Computer graphics, Jean-François Binet; **P.102 to 125**, Illustrations, Nicolas Hermlé.

Acknowledgements

The author and editor would particularly like to thank Christophe Bussien, Patrice Guinard, Lesler J. Ness (from Indiana University), Francis Santoni, Elizabeth Tessier and all the astrologers who provided valuable information to help us make this book a reality.

SATURN IN THE HOUSE OF TAURUS